From Your Friends At **The Mailbox**

JANUARY

A MONTH OF IDEAS AT YOUR FINGERTIPS!

GRADES 4–6

WRITTEN BY

Becky Andrews, Irving P. Crump, Ann Fisher, Peggy H. Hambright, Simone Lepine, Thad H. McLaurin, Darlene Parsons, Mary Lou Schlosser, Christine A. Thuman, Patricia Twohey, Chuck Westrick

EDITED BY

Becky Andrews, Lynn Bemer Coble,
Carol Rawleigh, Jennifer Rudisill, Gina Sutphin

ILLUSTRATED BY

Jennifer Tipton Bennett, Cathy Spangler Bruce, Pam Crane, Teresa Davidson, Clevell Harris, Rebecca Saunders, Barry Slate, Donna K. Teal

TYPESET BY

Lynette Maxwell, David Jarrell

COVER DESIGNED BY

Jennifer Tipton Bennett

www.themailbox.com

©1996 by THE EDUCATION CENTER, INC.
All rights reserved.

ISBN# 1-56234-140-5

Manufactured in the United States
10 9 8 7 6 5 4

TABLE OF CONTENTS

January Calendar

National Hot Tea Month

Tea is the only beverage in America commonly served hot or iced, anywhere, for any occasion. Have students research the history of tea. Where does it come from? How does it grow? What part has tea played in American history? Bring in a variety of flavored teas and let the students have a taste test.

Universal Letter-Writing Week

January 1–7 is a time for people all over the world to send letters and cards to friends and family. Have your students make new friends with kids in another city. Instruct each student to address an envelope with "Any Elementary School—Fourth (Fifth or Sixth) Grade Class." Then have him write the name of a city and state of his choice. (Don't forget the zip code!) Tell the student to use "Dear Fourth (Fifth or Sixth) Grade Student" as his greeting. Make sure the student requests a response. On a classroom map, track where letters are being sent with little red flags. Place a blue flag on the map when a response is received.

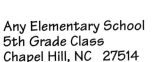

Tom Brown
444 Mill Dr.
Tulsa, OK 43251

Any Elementary School
5th Grade Class
Chapel Hill, NC 27514

4—Trivia Day

Celebrate all those interesting bits of information you've taught since August. Give each student an index card. Instruct the student to write one question about an interesting fact he's learned since the beginning of the year. Collect the cards and read the questions one by one to the class. Give each student who can correctly answer a question a treat.

Secret Pal Day

The second Sunday of January is Secret Pal Day. This is a day for secret pals to remember and do something special for each other. Put your students' names in a container and have each student draw one name (secret pal) from it. Instruct students not to buy gifts for their secret pals, but to do special deeds for them throughout the week. At the end of the week, have the secret pals reveal themselves to one another.

National Clean-Off-Your-Desk Day

This holiday is celebrated on the second Monday of January. Observe this day by having a "Classroom Clean-Up Day." Bring in lots of trash bags and have the kids do a little early spring cleaning. Give awards to students with the most organized, cleanest, or even messiest desks.

(Turn the page for more…)

11—Milkman Delivers First Bottle Of Milk

Milk in glass bottles was delivered for the first time on this day in 1878. Have students research to find out how milk was delivered before this. Ask students if milkmen still make home deliveries today. Most milk today comes in paper or plastic containers. Have students discuss the advantages and disadvantages of using paper and plastic instead of glass.

Hot And Spicy Food International Day

Hot and spicy food lovers of the world have a day of their own to celebrate (the third Saturday of January). On the Friday before this holiday, have students bring in their favorite hot and spicy dishes. Arrange the food buffet-style and let each student sample the different dishes. Before eating, have students share the names of their dishes and the countries from which they originated.

Backwards Day

Have your students celebrate Backwards Day on the last Friday of January. Encourage them to wear their clothes backwards, eat backwards (dessert first), and write their names backwards. Even arrange your daily schedule backwards!

28—Great Seal Of The United States Anniversary

On this day in 1782, Congress decided that the secretary of Congress should "keep the public seal, and cause the same to be affixed to every act, ordinance or paper, which Congress shall direct...." The seal had not been designed yet, but Congress recognized the need for a seal on this day. Have the students design a seal for your classroom or school. Discuss what might go on their seals (school founding date, school mascot, school motto, etc.). Let the students vote on the most appropriate seal for the classroom or school.

29—Freethinker's Day

This annual celebration is in honor of the birth of Thomas Paine, an American Revolutionary leader and author of *Common Sense* and *The Age of Reason*. Have your students observe this day by expressing their opinions about different issues in their community, state, or the nation. Read several examples of letters to the editor from your local or state newspaper; then have your students write their own letters to the editor.

Teacher's January Resource Calendar
A Handy List Of Special Days

January is named after the Roman god Janus and was originally the 11th month of the year. It was added to the ten-month Roman calendar (in around 700 B.C.), which began in March.

1 On this day in 1752, Betsy Ross—who is believed to have stitched the first stars-and-stripes flag under the instructions of George Washington—was born.

4 Louis Braille, the inventor of the touch system of reading and writing for the blind, was born on this day in 1809.

8 Elvis Presley, one of the most popular American singers in the history of rock music, was born on this day in 1935.

11 Amelia Earhart became the first woman to fly solo across the Pacific Ocean on this day in 1935.

13 The world's first wireless radio broadcast to the public took place on this day in 1910.

14 On this day in 1784, the Continental Congress ratified the Treaty of Paris, which officially ended the American Revolution and established the United States as a sovereign power.

15 Civil rights leader, minister, and Nobel Peace Prize winner Dr. Martin Luther King, Jr., was born on this day in 1929.

16 The U.S. National Aeronautics and Space Administration (NASA) accepted its first women candidates for astronauts on this day in 1978.

17 Benjamin Franklin—scientist, printer, publisher, diplomat, author, philosopher, philanthropist, and self-educated man—was born on this day in 1706.

18 Pooh Day is celebrated today in memory of A. A. Milne, the author of *Winnie The Pooh.* He was born on this day in 1882.

20 The first basketball game was played on this day in 1892 at a YMCA in Springfield, Massachusetts.

23 Elizabeth Blackwell became the first female in America to receive a medical degree on this day in 1849.

27 Wolfgang Amadeus Mozart, one of the world's greatest music makers, was born on this day in 1756.

31 Jackie Robinson, the first African-American to enter professional major-league baseball, was born on this day in 1919.

January Clip Art

Use on the following items:

- letters to parents
- games
- nametags
- notes to students
- homework assignments
- newsletters
- awards
- learning centers
- bulletin boards

HAPPY NEW YEAR!

United States

CLASSROOM TIMES

Teacher: _____ Date: _____

JANUARY

Highlights

Don't Forget!

Hats Off To...

Special Events

Help Wanted

FREE-TIME FUN for January!

Tackle these 20 terrific tasks when you finish your work.

Monday	Tuesday	Wednesday	Thursday	Friday
Paul Revere's warning is famous. How would Paul warn the patriots today? Write a story about Paul's ride as if it happened today. 	Alaska became the 49th state on January 3, 1959. List all the facts you know about the largest of the 50 states. 	George Washington Carver created more than 300 products from peanuts. List all the ways you've eaten peanuts.	January 24 is Reminiscence Day. Draw a picture of your earliest memory.	The *Eskimo Pie®*, a chocolate-covered ice-cream treat, was patented in 1922. Create your own new snack food.
Flip a coin. See if you can get tails more than four times in a row. It happens very rarely. 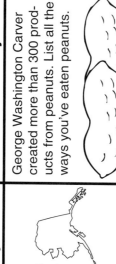	January 11 is International Thank You Day. Write a thank-you note to someone.	Amelia Earhart was the first woman to fly solo across the Pacific Ocean. Write about something you'd like to be the first to do. 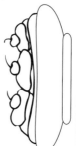	National Soup Month takes place in January. Name your favorite soup and list its ingredients.	For Read A New Book Month, critique a book you've just read. Rate the book using a four-star scale. (4 is the best!) 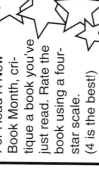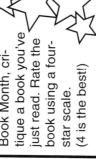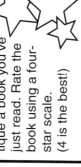
What's the strangest topping you've put on a hot dog? Make a list of unusual toppings that people might actually put on their hot dogs.	Create a magic square. Use each number 1–9 only once. The sum of each diagonal, horizontal, and vertical row must be the same. 1 3 7 4 6 5 8 2 9	How many six-letter words can you think of that have a four-letter word inside them? Examples: **SCARED** **SPORTS**	January 11 is Banana Split Day. Illustrate your favorite ice-cream dessert.	Super Bowl Sunday is in January. Did your team make it to the Super Bowl? Write a paragraph about your favorite team. 
Do you believe that life exists on other planets? Draw a picture showing how you think these life forms might look. 	How many five-letter words can you think of that have a three-letter word inside them? Examples: **FACES** **SCARE**	January is National Hobby Month. Describe your hobby or a hobby you would like to have.	Create a new candy bar. Draw a picture of your creation and describe it. **PHAT CANDY BAR**	Many authors use pen (false) names. Benjamin Franklin had 57 pen names. Create your own unique pen name. *Mark Twain* (A.K.A. Samuel Clemens)

Note To The Teacher: Have each student staple a copy of this page inside a file folder. Direct students to store their completed work inside their folders.

Desktag: Duplicate student copies on construction paper. Have each student personalize and decorate his pattern; then laminate the patterns and use them as desktags during January.

Award: Duplicate multiple copies. Keep them handy at your desk during the month of January. When a student earns an award, write the special activity earned on the appropriate lines. Or let the student choose the special activity with your approval.

©1996 The Education Center, Inc.

Ringing In The New Year

Thematic Activities For Welcoming A Brand-New Year

New Year's Day—probably the oldest holiday in the world—ushers in the beginning of a year full of new hopes and opportunities. Steer students toward making the most of the year ahead with this refreshing collection of activities.

by Peggy W. Hambright

New Year, what will
  you bring?
Three hundred sixty-five
  new opportunities?
A chance to start over
  again?
That's great! I need it!

Happy Birthday, New Year!

For thousands of years, people welcomed the new year in the spring—as some countries still do—because that's when nature comes to life again after the winter. Some religious groups—like the Jews, Muslims, and Hindus—set their own dates for celebrating the New Year. But most people recognize New Year's Day as the first day of January in each calendar year.

Have each student create a birthday card for the New Year. Ask the student to write a verse inside that's similar to a Japanese New Year's ode—a short poem consisting of just 31 syllables—as shown. Then string the birthday cards around your classroom door.

The Life And Times Of...The New Year

Ring in the New Year with a creative-writing project that chronicles the future year from infancy through retirement. Write the names of the 12 months across the chalkboard. Ask your students to brainstorm three or four major events that they predict will occur in each month of the new year. (Expect students to name catastrophes, kinds of weather, political changes, sporting events, new discoveries, inventions, etc.) As an event is named, list it under one of the months. Divide students into 12 groups; then assign each group a month. Ask each group to contribute an illustrated chapter that describes in detail the predicted events assigned to its month. When the chapters are complete, assemble them into a class book. Share a chapter each day with your class; then circulate the book for other classes to enjoy.

Good-Luck Fare

Does eating Hopping John (black-eyed peas cooked with rice) on New Year's Day bring good luck throughout the coming year? Many people believe that eating certain foods on New Year's Day brings good luck. Have students survey one another about the foods they and their families eat on New Year's Day to guarantee good fortune. Instruct students to show the collected data in picture graphs using appropriate symbols.

Keys To A Successful New Year

Unlock the door to a successful new year with this goal-setting bulletin board! Enlarge and color the five keys on page 15, programming them with the character traits shown. Arrange the keys on a bulletin board. Duplicate a copy of page 15 for each student. Direct each child to complete the identification tag for his key ring. Then have the student write two ways he plans to be successful in each area listed on the five keys. After each student has lightly colored, cut out, and hole-punched the keys, give him a length of colorful yarn on which to string them. Have the student loop the identification tag's flap over the yarn and glue it in place. Display the key rings on a bulletin board as shown.

11

A Look In Both Directions

Begin the first week in January by reflecting on the old year and looking ahead to the new one. Share with students that January was named after the Roman god Janus, who was believed to have had two faces—one that faced forward and looked to the future, and another that faced backward and looked at the past. Ask each student to ponder her life during the past year and what she hopes it will be like during the next 12 months. Give the student a 9" x 12" sheet of manila paper. Have her fold the paper in half, heading the left half "Looking Back" and the right half "Looking Ahead." Have the student list positive and negative actions she took last year in the left-hand column, and improvements she hopes to make this year in the right-hand column. Challenge the student to keep her paper until December 31 for a comparison!

Looking Back
Turned in most homework assignments on time.
Could have studied more for tests.
Was only late to school once.
Ate too much junk food.
Watched too much TV.

Looking Ahead
Turn in all homework on time.
Study harder for tests.
Return library books on time.
Go to bed without complaining.
Keep my room clean.

Happy New Year Around The World

Do people in other countries make confetti of old calendar pages and throw it out office windows like they do in San Francisco? Do they throw parties and make noise? Do they attend parades with flower-covered floats—like in Pasadena, California—or ones whose participants are mum—like in Philadelphia, Pennsylvania? How different *are* our New Year's customs from those of other countries? Ask each student or group to choose one or more of the countries listed on page 14. Let the student use a variety of library resources (or surf the Internet) to research additional information; then have her briefly summarize the custom(s) on an index card. Staple the students' cards around a world map on a bulletin board. Have each student match her card and country on the board by stapling a length of black yarn between them. Also ask the student to make a small, colored flag for the country she researched. Staple the flags around the perimeter of the board to make a colorful border.

Feed the dog.
Be kind to everyone.
Clean my room.
Talk on the phone less.
Go to bed when asked.
Improve my grades.
Complete all homework.
Watch less television.

Turnin' Over A New Leaf

Make it truly seem like New Year's by making noisemakers and resolutions. Ask each class member to place a handful of popcorn kernels or dried beans inside a toilet-tissue roll. Have the student wrap his roll with a 12" x 8" piece of Radiant Wrap (shiny, colorful sheets sold in craft stores), extending it beyond the ends. Direct the student to twist both ends closed and tie them with several lengths of colorful curling ribbon or Radiant Wrap shreds as shown. Ask the student to attach a card labeled with his resolutions to one end. Be sure to see "Toasting The New Year" on this page for a great way to share these resolutions.

Here We Go A-Wassailing

Stir up a warm and spicy fruit drink that's enjoyed at New Year's by folks in Scotland and merry old England. Combine the listed ingredients in a large pot and bring them to a boil. Cover the pot and let the mixture simmer for 20 minutes. Uncover and simmer 20 more minutes. Remove the spices. Serve the warm drink in student-decorated Styrofoam® cups during the "Toasting The New Year" activity on this page.

Wassail
2 quarts apple juice
2 1/4 cups pineapple juice
2 cups orange juice
1 cup lemon juice
1/2 cup sugar
1 teaspoon whole cloves
one three-inch stick of cinnamon
(Makes three quarts.)

Toasting The New Year

Wrap up your holiday study by making special celebratory toasts. Have the children sit in a circle holding their resolution noisemakers made in "Turnin' Over A New Leaf" and warm cups of wassail from "Here We Go A-Wassailing." Have the students take turns spinning a bottle (or an extra noisemaker) to see who is the first to share any one of his resolutions. After listening to the resolution, have everyone take one sip of wassail after raising their cups in unison and saying, "Here, here!" Direct the first person who shared to spin the bottle and determine who shares next. If the bottle points to someone who's already shared, ask the person to his right to share instead. When everyone has shared, have all of the students shout, "Happy New Year!" together and shake their resolution noisemakers!

New Year's Customs

Country	Custom
Bahamas	Participants—wearing strange and beautiful costumes of colorful crepe and tissue paper—march to calypso and goombay songs in the exciting Junkanoo parade.
Belgium	Farmers wish Happy New Year to their barnyard animals.
China	People enjoy a five-day festival with lion and dragon parades. They decorate pine and cypress branches with old coins and paper flowers, shoot off fireworks, and beat drums to frighten the old year away.
Denmark	People throw old pots, pans, and dishes at the doors of friends and play pranks similar to those done on Halloween in the United States.
Ecuador	Families burn a scarecrow and a will that represents the year's shortcomings.
England	People drink a hot, spicy drink called *wassail* from a bowl containing a good-luck ring. The one to drink from the cup with the ring will marry in the new year.
Former Soviet Union	Children visit the New Year Tree at the Kremlin Palace, see folk dancers perform, and get gifts from Grandfather Frost and Snow Maiden.
France	People eat pancakes to bring themselves good luck.
Germany	People sprinkle 12 onions with salt to predict whether the coming months will be wet or dry. They eat carp and save the scales to wear as good-luck charms.
Greece	Children receive cakes with a lucky coin baked inside each one; then at midnight they open gifts left in their shoes by St. Basil.
Hungary	Bells ring out across the land.
India	People cover the roofs of their houses, window ledges, and paths with small clay lamps during a five-day Festival of Lights.
Iran	Families watch to see if colored eggs sitting on mirrors move—proof that the earth shakes as the New Year begins.
Israel	Jews observe their New Year, Rosh Hashanah, at the end of summer or the beginning of autumn. They hear a ram's horn being blown, eat a bread called *challah,* and taste apple pieces dipped in honey.
Japan	People decorate their homes with pine, bamboo, and rope to bring good luck. They tie paper fortunes to trees, read cards from friends, and watch children unwrap packages of money from their parents.
Puerto Rico	Children dump pails of water out of windows at midnight to rid their homes of evil spirits.
Scotland	Families drink wassail and wait for their first visitor (or *first-footer*) to see whether he brings good or bad luck (based upon his hair color).
Spain	At midnight people eat one grape each time the clock strikes. This is supposed to bring good luck during each month of the new year.
Switzerland	People let a drop of cream fall on the floor for good luck.

Note To The Teacher: Use this list with "Happy New Year Around The World" on page 12.

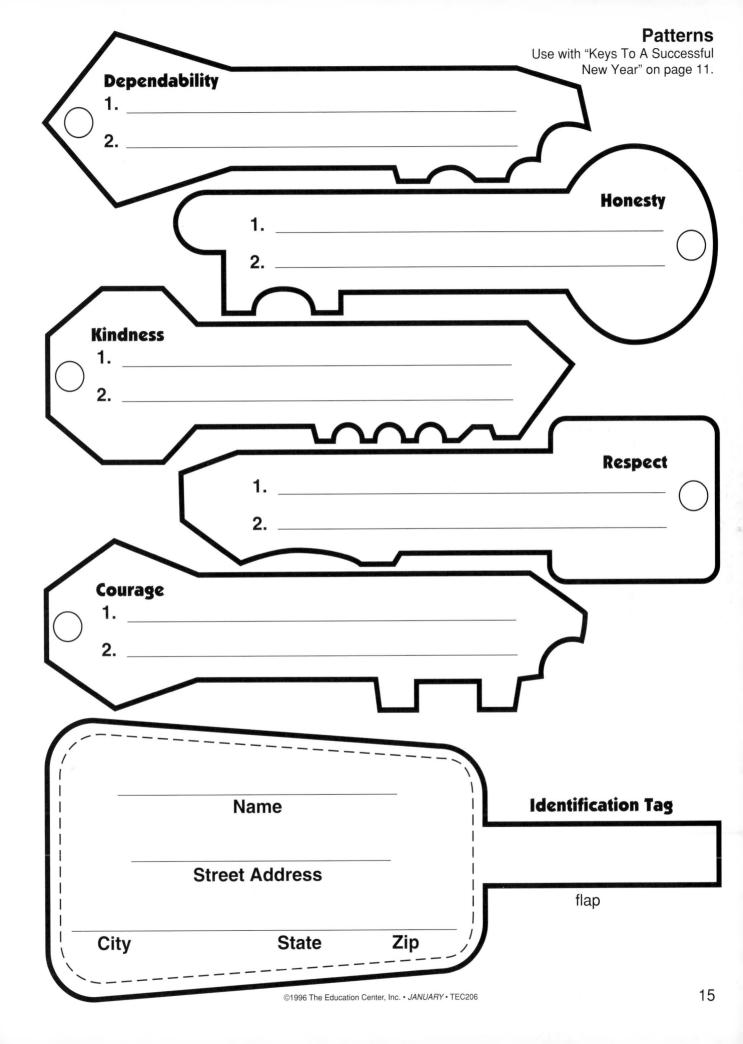

Dependability
1. _____
2. _____

Honesty
1. _____
2. _____

Kindness
1. _____
2. _____

Respect
1. _____
2. _____

Courage
1. _____
2. _____

_____
Name

Identification Tag

_____
Street Address

flap

City   **State**   **Zip**

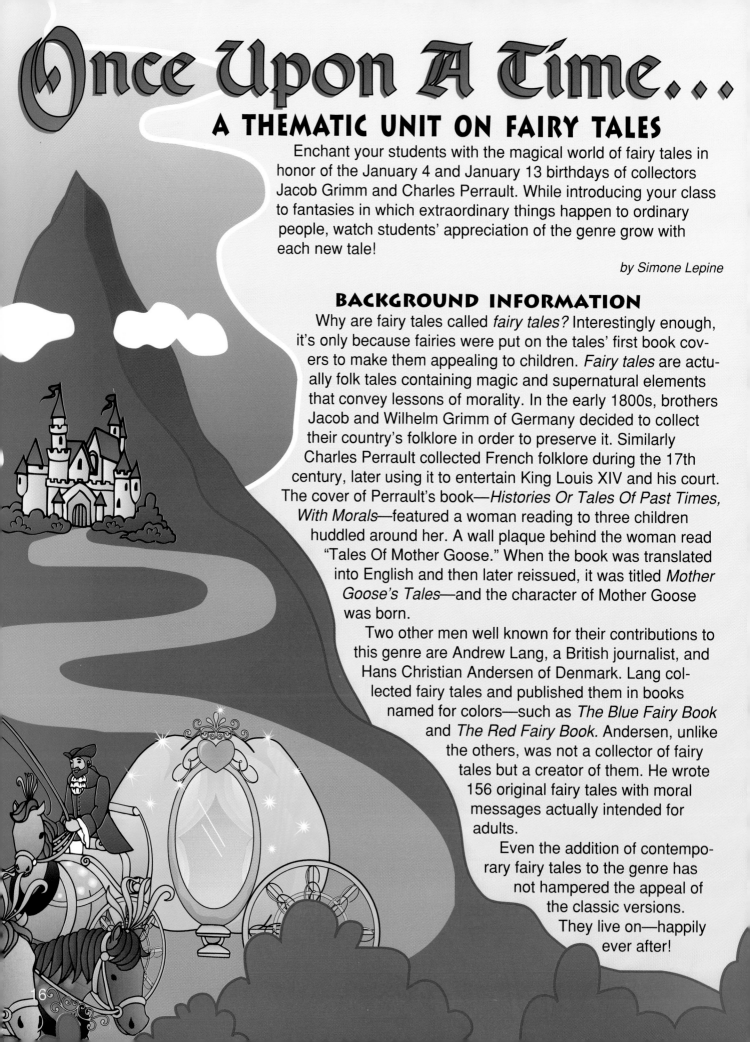

Once Upon A Time...

A THEMATIC UNIT ON FAIRY TALES

Enchant your students with the magical world of fairy tales in honor of the January 4 and January 13 birthdays of collectors Jacob Grimm and Charles Perrault. While introducing your class to fantasies in which extraordinary things happen to ordinary people, watch students' appreciation of the genre grow with each new tale!

by Simone Lepine

BACKGROUND INFORMATION

Why are fairy tales called *fairy tales?* Interestingly enough, it's only because fairies were put on the tales' first book covers to make them appealing to children. *Fairy tales* are actually folk tales containing magic and supernatural elements that convey lessons of morality. In the early 1800s, brothers Jacob and Wilhelm Grimm of Germany decided to collect their country's folklore in order to preserve it. Similarly Charles Perrault collected French folklore during the 17th century, later using it to entertain King Louis XIV and his court. The cover of Perrault's book—*Histories Or Tales Of Past Times, With Morals*—featured a woman reading to three children huddled around her. A wall plaque behind the woman read "Tales Of Mother Goose." When the book was translated into English and then later reissued, it was titled *Mother Goose's Tales*—and the character of Mother Goose was born.

Two other men well known for their contributions to this genre are Andrew Lang, a British journalist, and Hans Christian Andersen of Denmark. Lang collected fairy tales and published them in books named for colors—such as *The Blue Fairy Book* and *The Red Fairy Book.* Andersen, unlike the others, was not a collector of fairy tales but a creator of them. He wrote 156 original fairy tales with moral messages actually intended for adults.

Even the addition of contemporary fairy tales to the genre has not hampered the appeal of the classic versions. They live on—happily ever after!

WE'RE SWEET ON FAIRY TALES

Give your students a sweet reading incentive that becomes a colorful display! Mount the outline of a gingerbread house on a bulletin board as shown. Add a sugary trim to the house by gluing fiberfill to the roof's edges. Duplicate (enlarging if desired) a class supply of the candy patterns at the top of page 28. Have students color, cut out, and store the candy pieces at their desks. Every time a student reads a fairy tale, allow him to write his name and the title of the story on a piece of candy. Then have him attach the candy piece to the gingerbread house. The more students read, the sweeter the house will become! When the house is fully decorated, reward students by serving homemade gingerbread cookies. While students munch on their treats, read aloud the story of *Hansel And Gretel*, using one of the picture-book versions below.

SUGGESTED BOOKS:

Hansel And Gretel
by Jacob and Wilhelm Grimm
(Scholastic Inc., 1991)

Hansel And Gretel
retold by Rika Lesser
(The Putnam Publishing Group, 1989)

Hansel And Gretel
by James Marshall
(Dial Books For Young Readers, 1990)

Hansel And Gretel: The Witch's Story
by Sheila Black
(Carol Publishing Group, 1994)

PASSPORT TO FAIRY TALES

Expose your students to different world cultures by "visiting" different countries through fairy tales. Purchase a supply of inexpensive rubber stamps or stickers. Then supply each student with several copies of the reproducible passport at the bottom of page 29. Also give the student a copy of a world map and a sheet of construction paper to make a cover for his passport pages. Each time the student reads a fairy tale, have him fill out a passport page, attach a sticker (or get a stamp) from you to make it official, and color in the country from which the tale originated on his map. At the end of the unit, discuss with students how the tales from the countries they "visited" differed.

GRANTING WISHES

Everyone wishes for something from time to time, but rarely does the wish come true without action on our parts. Fairy-tale characters' wishes are granted right away—but with consequences or prices to pay. Read fairy-tale stories like "The Fisherman And His Wife," "Rumpelstiltskin," "The Foolish Wishes," and "The Poor Man And The Rich Man" with your class. Then have students complete the reproducible on page 33 to help them understand that getting what you want requires careful planning and hard work.

18

POP-UP BIOGRAPHIES

Enchanting fairy tales will be popping up everywhere with this fun cooperative-research activity. Divide your class into groups and assign each group a name of a folklorist from the list shown. Have each group find out when and where the folklorist lived and which tales were published by him. Arm students with encyclopedias and other resources to conduct their research. Point out that the introduction to a book of fairy tales often includes information about its author/collector. Give each group two pieces of 8 1/2" x 11" paper, glue, scissors, colored pencils, paper scraps, and the directions below for making the pop-up biography. Have each group display its completed pop-up biography at a center or in your school's media center.

MAJOR FOLKLORISTS:

Charles Perrault
Jacob and Wilhelm Grimm
Andrew Lang
Peter Christian Asbjørnsen
Joseph Jacobs

DIRECTIONS FOR EACH GROUP:

1. Fold one of the papers in half. Cut two 2-inch slits three inches apart in the center of the folded edge (figure 1).
2. Fold the center section down, creasing it at the bottom of the cuts; then bend the section back to its original position (figure 2).
3. Push the center section to the inside of the folded paper. Crease the folds again so that they bend in opposite directions, making the center section pop out like a table (figure 3).
4. Place the other piece of paper behind the first; then glue it in place (figure 4).

5. Make a miniature book from small scraps of paper. On the cover of the miniature book, write the title of a story or book your person published.
6. Glue the miniature book to the pop-up section of your card (figure 5).
7. Lay the card flat. Label the top portion of it with your folklorist's name. Write interesting facts about the folklorist around the pop-up portion (figure 5).

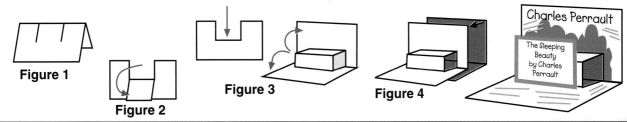

Figure 1

Figure 2

Figure 3

Figure 4

Figure 5

Charles Perrault

The Sleeping Beauty by Charles Perrault

Rumpelstiltskin is my name!

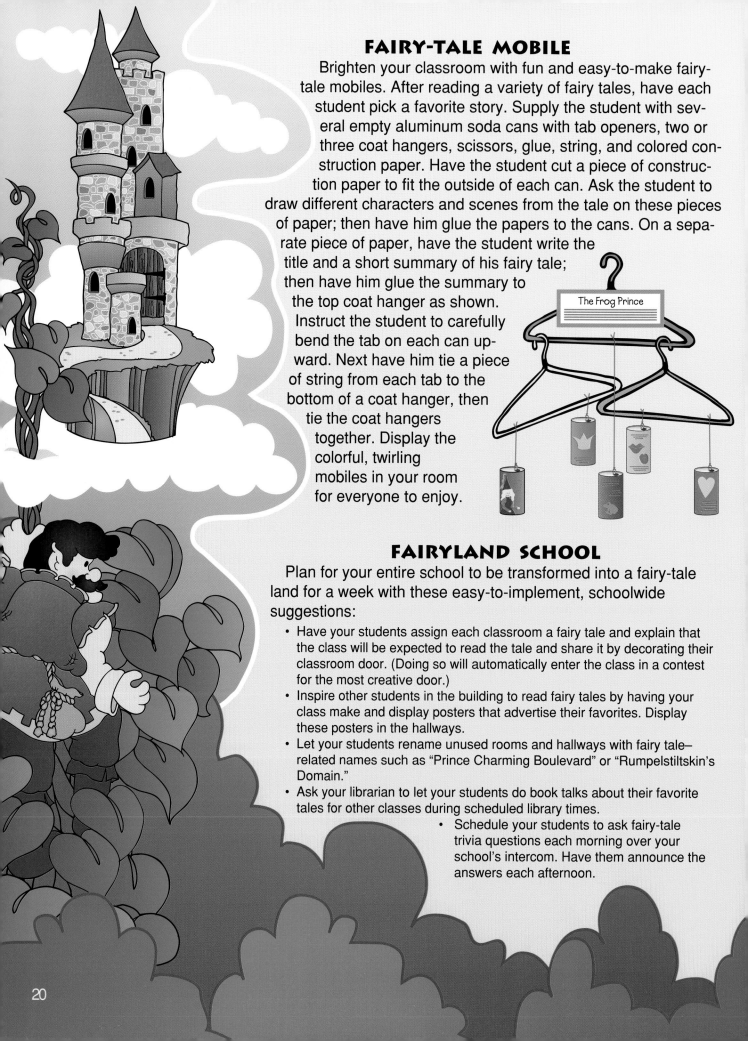

FAIRY-TALE MOBILE

Brighten your classroom with fun and easy-to-make fairy-tale mobiles. After reading a variety of fairy tales, have each student pick a favorite story. Supply the student with several empty aluminum soda cans with tab openers, two or three coat hangers, scissors, glue, string, and colored construction paper. Have the student cut a piece of construction paper to fit the outside of each can. Ask the student to draw different characters and scenes from the tale on these pieces of paper; then have him glue the papers to the cans. On a separate piece of paper, have the student write the title and a short summary of his fairy tale; then have him glue the summary to the top coat hanger as shown. Instruct the student to carefully bend the tab on each can upward. Next have him tie a piece of string from each tab to the bottom of a coat hanger, then tie the coat hangers together. Display the colorful, twirling mobiles in your room for everyone to enjoy.

The Frog Prince

FAIRYLAND SCHOOL

Plan for your entire school to be transformed into a fairy-tale land for a week with these easy-to-implement, schoolwide suggestions:

- Have your students assign each classroom a fairy tale and explain that the class will be expected to read the tale and share it by decorating their classroom door. (Doing so will automatically enter the class in a contest for the most creative door.)
- Inspire other students in the building to read fairy tales by having your class make and display posters that advertise their favorites. Display these posters in the hallways.
- Let your students rename unused rooms and hallways with fairy tale–related names such as "Prince Charming Boulevard" or "Rumpelstiltskin's Domain."
- Ask your librarian to let your students do book talks about their favorite tales for other classes during scheduled library times.
- Schedule your students to ask fairy-tale trivia questions each morning over your school's intercom. Have them announce the answers each afternoon.

FAIRY-TALE ADVICE COLUMN

Move over, Ann Landers! You're being replaced with the Fairy Godmother! Review letter writing with your class. Have each student take on the persona of a fairy-tale protagonist; then have him write a letter to an advice columnist requesting help with a particular problem. Ask the student to then "mail" the letter to a partner who—in the role of the advice columnist—answers and returns the letter to its writer. Require that the advice be realistic, allowing no magical solutions. Let students share some of their responses with the class.

CLASS(IC) FAIRY TALE

Nurture cooperation by having the class write an add-on fairy tale. Using the list below as a guide, discuss with students the different elements that a fairy tale can have. Then, as a class, establish the tale's setting, describe the good and bad characters, and define the problem. Next explain that each student will write three to five sentences of the story, leaving his part open-ended enough so that the next person who writes can add to it. Also tell students that it's permissible to interject minor characters, such as people passing along the road or talking animals, to extend the story. After each student writes his story part, have him discuss what's been written with the next student and suggest what he foresees happening next. Plan for a certain number of students to write each day; then continue the activity over several days until all students have had a chance to contribute to the tale.

Dear Fairy Godmother,
My stepmother is so mean to me. She makes me do all the work while my stepsisters sit around and do nothing. Next week is the Prince's Great Ball, and I have to sit home and do chores while they all get to go and have fun! Please tell me what I can do so I can go, too!

Sincerely yours,
Cinderella
(a.k.a. Susy Smith)

FAIRY TALES:
- Begin with phrases like "Once upon a time…"
- Take place long ago and in faraway places
- Usually have young heroes and heroines whose virtues help them overcome obstacles
- Have a good character and a bad character
- Use characters with unusual names
- Have the good character pass several tests or overcome many trials in order to solve a problem
- Always allow the good character to win and be rewarded
- Always see that the bad character loses and is punished for his deeds
- Involve magic and supernatural happenings
- Don't have to include fairy characters
- Sometimes allow characters to be transformed into animals or to come under spells that only acts of kindness or love can reverse
- Often have royal characters such as kings and queens
- Have a series of events that happens or several tests that the hero/heroine must pass
- Use numbers such as three and seven (three wishes, seven pigs, etc.)
- Have happy endings so that the characters live "happily ever after"

IT'S ALL IN THE WAY YOU SAY IT

Help students understand that fairy tales were originally for telling aloud by having them create and record original fairy tales. Duplicate the reproducible planning sheet on page 30 for each child. Remind students to incorporate the literary elements of a fairy tale given on page 21 as they complete these written plans. Explain that their stories can be similar to existing ones since many fairy tales borrow certain elements, characters, and plots from each other. Have each student tape-record himself sharing his tale on a cassette tape. Place the tapes at a listening center.

Vary this activity by having one student at a time listen to a taped tale and then retell it from memory to the class. This activity is sure to help students understand why there are so many different versions of the same story.

FAIRY-TALE DEBATES

Who is the worst villain in fairy tales? Which hero or heroine has the worst situation to overcome? Allow your students to debate these two questions within groups. First read aloud three or four fairy tales that have strong villain/hero/heroine conflicts (see the booklist on this page). Make a sign with the title of each tale that you read; then place a sign in each corner of your classroom. Next ask students to stand in the corner with the tale that they believe had the worst villain. Once groups have formed in this way, have the students within each group agree on the reasons for their choice and share them with the class.

Form the next round of debate teams by asking students to stand in the corner of the tale in which they think the hero/heroine had the worst situation to overcome. Follow the same procedure as before. After the debates, encourage students to share other fairy-tale characters and situations that have memorable villains or problems to solve. Be sure to see the reproducible—"Most-Wanted Villain"—at the top of page 29 for a great follow-up.

SUGGESTED BOOKS:

The Great Quillow
by James Thurber
(Harcourt Brace & Company, 1994)

The Sleeping Beauty: A Fairy Tale
by Jacob and Wilhelm Grimm
translated by Anthea Bell
(North-South Books, 1995)

Little Red-Cap
by Jacob and Wilhelm Grimm
translated by Anthea Bell
(North-South Books, 1995)

The Three Billy Goats Gruff
by Tim Arnold
(Simon & Schuster Children's Books, 1993)

FAIRY-TALE MAPS

What if the woods of Little Red Riding Hood were next to Sleeping Beauty's castle or near Rumpelstiltskin's hut? Inject some map skills into your fairy-tale study by having student groups create maps that incorporate the settings of several different tales. Divide the class into groups of four or five students. Have each group member read a different fairy tale. Then give each group a large sheet of newsprint (or white construction paper), crayons or markers, and a copy of the following directions:

DIRECTIONS FOR EACH GROUP:

1. Ask every member of the group to share his fairy tale's plot and setting.
2. Together create a map of a new land that includes the setting of each group member's tale.
3. Label all important places or physical features, such as mountains or rivers.
4. Design a map key.
5. Discuss ways your characters could interact if they really were neighbors. Decide who would be friends and enemies.
6. Based on your discussion, write a cooperative tale that could take place in your map's fairy-tale land.

Schedule times for each group to present its new fairy tale to the group and show its map. After all groups have shared, compile the groups' maps into a fairy-tale atlas for the whole class to enjoy.

FAMILY FOLKLORIST

Give each student a taste of what being a folklorist is like by allowing her to become one. Have each student ask an adult she knows to tell his or her favorite fairy tale to her. Direct the student to write down the tale as it's being told to her as exactly as she can. Discourage the student from tape-recording the story, since neither Perrault nor the Brothers Grimm had the convenience of a recorder.

After the interview, quiz the student on what she learned about writing a story this way. Does she think the tale changed from its telling to its writing? How does she think that writing stories this way could lead to having different versions of the same tale? Are there parts of the tale that she would have told differently if she could? Why does she think folklorists try to write the stories they collect as nearly like the spoken tales as possible? After discussing these questions with your students, compile their stories into a class book that they can read during free time.

AND THEY WIN HAPPILY EVER AFTER

Turn students into future Milton Bradleys by having them convert fairy tales into creative board games. Divide students into groups; then give each group a set of markers and a sheet of poster board. Have each group create a board game that reviews a fairy tale's sequence of events as it's being played. Ask students to insert spaces with messages like "The wolf has a tummyache. Miss a turn." Then set aside a special day for the students to play each other's games.

DIARY OF OPPOSING CHARACTERS

How often have you told your students that there are two sides to every story? Let students experience different characters' perspectives through a diary-writing activity. Remind students that a fairy tale's plot usually revolves around the good character versus the bad character, with the good character prevailing. But what if what was written represented only one side of the story? As an example, share *The True Story Of The Three Little Pigs!* as told to Jon Scieszka (Viking Children's Books, 1989)—a story told from the wolf's perspective.

Ask each student to select any fairy-tale incident that pits the good character against the bad one. Then have the student pretend she is the good character and write a diary entry describing the event from that perspective. Next have her pretend that she is the bad character. This time ask the student to describe the same event from the bad character's point of view—supplying any information that the good character left out of the original story!

WALT DISNEY VS. THE BROTHERS GRIMM

Is Walt Disney's version of *Snow White* the only one your students are familiar with? If so, they probably aren't alone. Help students discover the differences between fairy tales and their video versions with this activity. First have students bring in empty cereal boxes. Ask students to brainstorm a list of fairy tales that they've seen on television, at the movie theater, or on video as you write the titles on the board. Give each student scissors, glue, assorted art supplies, and a copy of the pattern at the bottom of page 28. Have him cut off the top flaps of the box and then cover and decorate the cereal box to look like a television set. Next ask the student to write one of the titles listed earlier on his pattern and glue it to his box. After each student has made his television, help him locate a book that includes his tale. Have students read their tales. Then discuss with them how the written tales differ from the video versions. Ask, "Which parts were left out or changed? How were they the same?" After the discussion, have each child place his tale (or a duplicated copy of it) inside his box. Display the televisions in the classroom, encouraging students to read the stories during free time.

LEARNING YOUR LESSON

What are some of the valuable lessons taught through fairy tales? Could a character have avoided a bad situation by behaving better? Did a character's goodness help him prevail against adversity? Let students investigate some of the morals taught by fairy tales. First help each student select a tale that teaches a clear lesson. Then give the student a copy of the reproducible on page 31 to help her analyze the tale and discover its lesson. Afterwards allow students to share the lessons that were gleaned from the tales. Assist students with grouping similar lessons into categories. Question students about whether the lessons from fairy tales are relevant for today. Then ask what kinds of lessons they think modern fairy tales should teach. Follow up this activity with "Prince Charming, Where Are You?" on page 26.

PRINCE CHARMING, WHERE ARE YOU?

The typical fairy tale portrays a princess or a damsel in distress who is rescued by a dashing prince. But ladies in modern stories are not always saved by knights in shining armor. Set the stage for this writing activity by sharing *The Paper Bag Princess* by Robert Munsch (Firefly Books, Ltd.; 1980), a book in which the princess has to save the prince. Then select a fairy tale for class members to rewrite. Brainstorm and list ideas with students about which parts need to be changed in order to make it a modernized version: names, setting, social conditions, clothing, transportation, job descriptions, attitudes toward women, etc. Then have each student write an updated version of the tale to share with the class.

HAVEN'T I HEARD THIS STORY BEFORE?

Was Little Red Riding Hood eaten by the wolf? Or was she saved by a hunter who cut her out of the wolf's stomach? Point out to students that fairy tales have similar versions. In fact, the Cinderella story has more than 360 known versions! Students won't find this hard to believe once you remind them that fairy tales were originally passed down by word of mouth from generation to generation before ever being written down. Emphasize that the more students read fairy tales, the more they'll recognize familiar themes.

Challenge each student to find two versions of the same fairy tale; then have him complete the reproducible on page 32. Or select two versions from the list below to read aloud; then have the class complete the reproducible together.

SUGGESTED TALES:

"The Tale Of The Snowmaiden" from *Koshka's Tales: Stories From Russia* by James Mayhew (Kingfisher LKC, 1993) to compare with Hans Christian Andersen's *The Snow Queen* retold by Caroline Peachey (Harcourt Brace & Company, 1994)

The Irish Cinderlad by Shirley Climo (HarperCollins Pubs. Inc:, 1996) or *Sootface: An Ojibwa Indian Tale* retold by Robert D. San Souci (Doubleday & Company, Inc.; 1994) to compare with Charles Perrault's *Cinderella* translated by Marcia Brown (Simon & Schuster Children's Books, 1988)

"The Bee, The Harp, The Mouse, And The Bum-Clock" from *Favorite Fairy Tales Told In Ireland* by Virginia Haviland, edited by Amy Cohn (William Morrow & Co., Inc:, 1994) to compare with *Jack And The Beanstalk* retold by Steven Kellogg (Morrow Junior Books, 1991)

"A Frog's Gift" from *Mysterious Tales Of Japan* by Rafe Martin (G. P. Putnam's Sons, 1996) to compare with Jacob and Wilhelm Grimms' *The Frog Prince* retold by Edith H. Tarcov (Scholastic Inc., 1993)

"FAIR-LY" TRIVIAL MATTERS

"Who was the girl who lost her glass slipper? On how many mattresses did the princess sleep?" Sharpen students' recall with trivia questions like these to review the fairy tales they've read. Have each student make one or more trivia cards by writing a question at the top of an index card. Instruct the student to cut a "window" near the bottom of the card and tape the question's answer behind it. Store the trivia cards in a decorated file box for students to use individually or as a team game. When your fairy-tale unit is completed, share the game with other classes or donate it to the school library.

FAIRY-TALE ARTIFACTS

Spark your students' creative-thinking skills with an activity that reviews the fairy tales read and discussed in class. Have each student fill a shoe box with items or pictures that represent clues to a favorite fairy tale. For example, filling a box with long braids, a skein of silk (yarn), stones, and thorns could represent the story of Rapunzel. Have the student present the box to the class—keeping the identity of the fairy tale a secret—as proof that the story's character really existed and the events truly happened. Have the class try to guess the title of the student's fairy tale. Once the story has been guessed, let the student archaeologist tell about her collection of "unearthed" artifacts.

Q: Who lost a glass slipper?

A: Cinderella

jennifer bennett

Patterns

Use with "We're Sweet On Fairy Tales" on page 17.

Pattern

Use with "Walt Disney Vs. The Brothers Grimm" on page 25.

Most-Wanted Villain

Reward: _____

Villain's Description:

_____

_____

_____

_____

_____

_____

_____

_____

_____

Villain's Crime:

_____

_____

_____

_____

_____

_____

_____

_____

Name Of Villain:

_____

Name Of Fairy Tale In Which Crime Occurred: _____

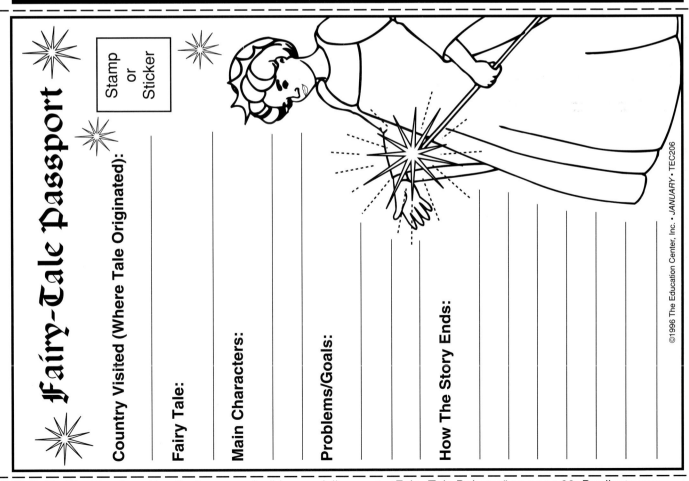

Fairy-Tale Passport

Country Visited (Where Tale Originated):

Stamp
or
Sticker

Fairy Tale:

Main Characters:

Problems/Goals:

How The Story Ends:

Note To The Teacher: Use the top reproducible as a follow-up to "Fairy-Tale Debates" on page 22. Duplicate one copy for each student to use in making a "Most-Wanted Villain" miniposter to display. Have the student draw a picture of the villain inside the frame. Use the bottom reproducible with "Passport To Fairy Tales" on page 18.

Name _____

Writing And Telling A Fairy Tale

Fairy tales are actually folktales that contain magical and unusual happenings. They were originally told by word of mouth to entertain or teach lessons. The fairy tales we read today were collected by such folklorists as Charles Perrault and the Brothers Grimm. These men interviewed the storytellers, listened to their tales, and then wrote the stories they heard as exactly as they could.

Fill in the guide below to help you plan your own fairy tale to write or share orally.

Title

_____

Setting
(Long ago and in a faraway place)

Place:

_____

Time:

_____

Good Character
(Usually a young person with an unusual name)

Name:

_____

Description:

_____

_____

_____

_____

Bad Character
(Usually a villain with an unusual name)

Name:

_____

Description:

_____

_____

_____

_____

Problem (A magical or unusual happening—like a spell that changes a person or thing into something else—that can be reversed only by true love or a kind deed):

_____

_____

_____

Happy Ending (How the good character wins and the villain is punished):

_____

_____

_____

Events (Several events that happen or tests that must be passed while the problem is being solved):

1. _____

2. _____

3. _____

4. _____

5. _____

6. _____

7. _____

Note To The Teacher: Use this reproducible with "It's All In The Way You Say It!" on page 22. Duplicate one copy for each student.

Name _____

Learning A Lesson

Fairy tales were meant to entertain, but many were also meant to teach a lesson or an important rule to follow. Sometimes a character gets into trouble for behaving badly or gets rewarded for being good. Sometimes characters fall into trouble because they do not listen to warnings. See if you can find a fairy tale's hidden lesson by completing the activity below.

_____

Title of fairy tale

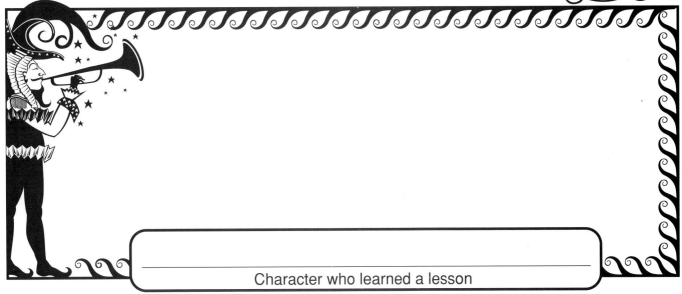

_____
Character who learned a lesson

Describe the character's actions or behavior in the story. _____
_____
_____
_____
_____
_____
_____
_____
_____

What happens to the character because of his or her actions or behavior? _____
_____
_____
_____
_____
_____
_____
_____

What lesson does the character learn?_____
_____
_____

Bonus Box: Pick a rule that you have to obey either at home or at school. Create a fairy tale that will teach others to follow that rule.

Note To The Teacher: Use this reproducible with "Learning Your Lesson" on page 25. Duplicate one copy for each student. Have the student draw a picture of the character who learned a lesson inside the box.

Copycats?

Many versions of the same fairy tale exist. But even though their story lines are similar, they do contain differences. Summarize two versions of the same tale in the boxes below. Then cut only along the dotted lines to form doors that open from the center outward. Fold the doors so that they open. Tape or staple another sheet of paper behind the door openings. On the paper behind the doors, write about how the two tales are similar and different. Then answer the questions at the bottom of the page.

Fold

Title _____

Author _____

_____
_____
_____
_____
_____
_____
_____
_____
_____
_____

Title _____

Author _____

_____
_____
_____
_____
_____
_____
_____
_____
_____
_____

Fold

1. Which version do you like better? _____

2. Why do you like this version more? _____

_____

3. Why do you think there are different versions of this story? _____

_____

4. How would you change the story if you were going to tell it? _____

_____

Bonus Box: Rewrite the story on another sheet of paper the way *you* would tell it.

Note To The Teacher: Use this reproducible with "Haven't I Heard This Story Before?" on page 26. Duplicate one copy for each student. Provide the student with scissors, a stapler or tape, and another sheet of 8 1/2" x 11" paper.

32

Granting Wishes

Have you ever wished for something that came true? How would you like to have three wishes? In fairy tales, characters are often granted three wishes. Sometimes, though, a character—like the wife in "The Fisherman And His Wife"—finds that she's better off having no wishes at all!

On the lines below, write some of the wishes you would make if you were given this magical chance. Ask for things that you want for yourself, your family, and the world. Your wishes can be for realistic things like toys or feelings like courage or love. But you can't wish for more wishes! Then answer the questions at the bottom of the page.

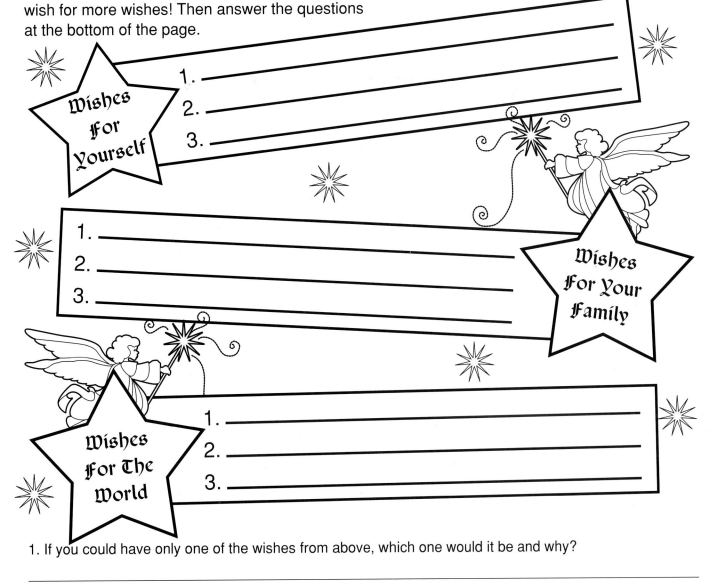

Wishes For Yourself
1. _____
2. _____
3. _____

1. _____
2. _____
3. _____
Wishes For Your Family

Wishes For The World
1. _____
2. _____
3. _____

1. If you could have only one of the wishes from above, which one would it be and why?

_____

_____

2. Since fairy-tale magic doesn't exist, what could you do to make this wish come true?

_____

_____

_____

Bonus Box: Grant someone else's wish! Find out about a wish that a parent, a close relative, a friend, or a teacher has. Write this person a note explaining how you want to help make the wish come true.

Note To The Teacher: Use this reproducible with "Granting Wishes" on page 18. Duplicate one copy for each student. In "The Fisherman And His Wife," the wife's greed compels her to keep asking for bigger and better things. At the end of the story, she has nothing more than she had at the beginning.

A Man For His Time

A Thematic Unit About Dr. Martin Luther King, Jr.

He was a man for his time—committed to pursuing his dream of equality for all. Develop an atmosphere of cooperation and increase appreciation for the national day that remembers Dr. Martin Luther King, Jr., with this creative collection of activities.

by Mary Lou Schlosser and Peggy W. Hambright

Happy Birthday To You!

Celebrate the birthday of Dr. Martin Luther King, Jr., with a unique critical-thinking activity. First separately wrap the lid and bottom of a box with birthday paper. Add a colorful bow to the lid. Next read aloud one of the following books:

Happy Birthday, Martin Luther King by Jean Marzollo (Scholastic Inc., 1993)

Martin Luther King by Rosemary L. Bray (Greenwillow Books, 1995)

Martin Luther King, Jr. by Kathie B. Smith (Silver Burdett Press, 1987)

With the wrapped box on display, ask each class member to think of a gift he would like to have given Dr. King. Ask the student to describe his gift idea in a paragraph; then—as he comes to place it inside the gift box—have him share with the class why his gift is an appropriate one for Dr. King.

Peace By Piece

Reconstruct the life of Dr. Martin Luther King, Jr., through a class quilt-making project. Duplicate page 42; then cut apart the pieces on the grid. Give one piece to each student. Have him use encyclopedias, library books, or computer-generated information to research the facts that will answer his square's question. After researching, have the student write a summary—including an illustration—on a white paper square. Ask the student to glue his white square to a larger square of colored tagboard. Help students arrange all of the individual squares into one large square or rectangle, ordering the squares sequentially so that they retell Dr. King's life story. After the squares have been arranged, have students hole-punch the sides of the squares. Then give students yarn for "stitching" the squares together to create a class quilt. Display the completed quilt on a wall for all to enjoy.

Jump Aboard The Literature Connection

Design a unique bulletin board that helps students broaden their understanding of the freedom and equality themes espoused by Dr. King. Gather and display books like the ones listed below and in "Happy Birthday To You!" on page 34. Enlarge the engine and train-car patterns from page 47, making one car for each featured book. Write a book title on each train car. For each book, label an index card with questions that can be answered by skimming the book. Arrange the engine, the train cars, and a construction-paper track on a bulletin board as shown. Staple each train car on three sides to make a pocket; then insert the matching activity card inside the pocket. Challenge students to practice their reading skills during free time by answering the cards' questions.

Suggested Books:
Teammates by Peter Golenbock (Harcourt Brace & Company, 1990)
The Story Of Ruby Bridges by Robert Coles (Scholastic Inc., 1995)
The Black Snowman by Phil Mendez (Scholastic Inc., 1989)
Just Like Martin by Ossie Davis (Simon & Schuster Children's Books, 1992)
The Year They Walked: Rosa Parks & The Montgomery Bus Boycott by Beatrice Siegel (Simon & Schuster Children's Books, 1992)
The March On Washington by James S. Haskins (HarperCollins Children's Books, 1993)
Talking Walls by Margy B. Knight (Tilbury House, Publishers; 1992)

Young Crusaders

Instill in children that they—like Dr. Martin Luther King, Jr.—can impact our world. Share ways that young people have made a difference by reading excerpts from *Witnesses To Freedom: Young People Who Fought For Civil Rights* by Belinda Rochelle (Dutton Children's Books, 1993). Ask students to bring in newspaper or magazine articles (or summarized television accounts) of instances when children have brought about positive changes. Then have each student write a news article that tells about herself one year from now. What is she doing that's making a difference? Is she helping a particular group? Why? Will she be honored for her involvement or accomplishments? Allow students to share their stories aloud.

I'll Remember You

People of distinction—like Dr. Martin Luther King, Jr.—are remembered for their accomplishments in different ways. Naming cities, buildings, streets, and parks for important people is just one of the ways that our society honors others. Have students collectively list Dr. King's character traits and accomplishments. Then instruct each class member to become a part of this scenario: "A new building [or street or park] in your town is to be named in honor of Dr. King. Lots of important people have been invited to attend its official dedication. You have been asked to make the introductory speech." Have each student study the list that the class compiled to help him decide what to say about Dr. King. Then have the student compose a speech that would be appropriate for the occasion. After the speeches have been written, allow class members to present them to the class.

About Violence

Martin Luther King once spoke of "…the self-defeating effects of physical violence." Explain to students the meaning of Dr. King's quote—that a person who commits violence against others never benefits personally from it. Let students discuss the meanings of the term *violence.* Then ask each student to respond to one of the following questions in his journal:

- Why do you think violence occurs today?
- What thoughts and feelings do you have when you hear or read about a violent act?
- What are your opinions on violence in today's schools?
- What are some positive ways people can stop violence today?

Let volunteers share their writings with the class.

About Peace

Dr. King once said, "Sooner or later all the people of the world will have to discover a way to live together in peace…." Allow students to symbolically represent this concept by making a cooperative display. From tagboard cut 12-inch letters that spell the word PEACE. Divide students into five groups; then give each group one of the letters and several old newspapers, magazines, photos, or printed sheets of computer-generated clip art. Let each group cut out and glue pictures of as many different kinds of people as possible to its letter to make a colorful collage. Display the decorated letters on a bulletin board along with Dr. King's quote.

Save our environment.

Help homeless children.

Help kids with AIDS.

Moved To March

In one of Dr. King's speeches, he inspires his listeners to march in support of ideas and causes in which they believe. Allow your students to "march" for something they support. Duplicate a class supply of the marcher patterns on page 46. Have each student decorate a marcher to represent himself, then cut out the pattern. Then have each student cut out a brick shape from a red sheet of construction paper. On his brick, have the student list (or draw a picture of) a cause or an idea about which he feels strongly enough to march. Display the figures—marching on a road of student-made bricks—on a classroom wall.

Many Sides To One Issue

Like Dr. King, other African-Americans have worked for civil rights—but each had his or her own idea about the best way to achieve them. Have students conduct research to compare the beliefs and strategies of Dr. Martin Luther King, Jr., with those of Malcolm X and Marcus Garvey.

As students will discover during their research, Dr. King, Malcolm X, and Marcus Garvey all had different opinions about how to gain civil rights. Guide students to conclude that even though there are different possible solutions, some are better than others. Divide students into groups; then give each group an index card labeled with a conflict (see the list below). Ask the group to brainstorm three solutions for its conflict along with possible consequences. After having each group role-play two of its solutions for the entire class, poll the class to determine the better alternative.

- Your coach needs you at practice to prepare for tomorrow night's big game, but practice for the school's music concert is scheduled at the same time.
- A group of older kids is teasing your younger brother/sister about wearing glasses.
- You and one other group member completed all of the group's assignment, while the other two members talked and contributed nothing.
- You don't understand a science chapter, and you've just had an argument with your study buddy. You need to pass the next test.
- You and your brother share responsibility for cleaning up each night after dinner. You've been invited to spend Friday and Saturday nights with a friend. Your brother is complaining that he'll have the job by himself for two nights.
- The teacher is upset that someone let the hamster out of its cage. You know who was responsible.

A Lesson From Turmoil

Dr. Martin Luther King, Jr., was familiar with the unrest associated with important issues like civil rights. Even so, he realized that something good can come from even the worst of situations. Make this point with students by sharing Eve Bunting's *Smoky Night* (Harcourt Brace & Company, 1994). This book beautifully illustrates—in the midst of riots and looting—the value of getting along with others, regardless of nationality or background. After sharing the book, have each student write a story about a valuable lesson he or she learned during an unstable or fearful situation. Provide a time for volunteers to share their stories.

Profile Of Courage

Tremendous inner strength is required of people like Dr. King who are willing to stand apart to achieve a desired goal. Help students imagine what it's like to forge ahead on an important issue—sometimes alone—when strong beliefs compel you to persist and endure. Share with your class the story of the first black child to attend an all-white elementary school by reading *The Story Of Ruby Bridges* by Robert Coles (Scholastic Inc., 1995). Have students brainstorm a list of qualities that a person must possess in order to withstand the pressures of striving toward a challenging goal (for example, courage, perseverance, etc.).

Then divide students into groups. Ask each group to write a skit about someone who is working toward a difficult goal. Instruct students that each skit should include a character whose strong convictions require one or more of the qualities they listed earlier. After the skits have been presented, compile them into a class book titled "Profiles Of Courage."

Different Strokes For Different Folks

Civil rights leaders like Dr. Martin Luther King, Jr., favored the use of nonviolent strategies. But those he promoted were not the nonviolent ones of petition-signing and letter-writing so often endorsed. Instead he encouraged *marches, boycotts, sit-ins, wade-ins,* and *stand-ins*. Help students investigate these new terms and why they are so effective by sharing *If You Lived At The Time Of Martin Luther King* by Ellen Levine (Scholastic Inc., 1990). To contrast Dr. King's nonviolent strategies with other standard ones, have groups of students list situations that could be changed more effectively by using one of Dr. King's methods instead of petition-signing or letter-writing. List their examples on chart paper divided into two columns as shown. Help students understand that—while both kinds of strategies are nonviolent forms of direct action—one demands attention while the other does not.

Use Dr. King's Strategies	Use Letters/Petitions
Stop cutting down a tree. Stop violence on TV by boycotting advertisers on violent shows.	Encourage Congress to spend more on education.

Dear Dr. King

Foster creative problem-solving abilities in your youngsters by continuing the example set by Martin Luther King, Jr. Transform a shoebox into a collection bin for "Dear Dr. King" letters. Explain that students are to write letters to Dr. King soliciting his advice on how to solve problems they are currently experiencing. In the student's letter, have him briefly describe the problem without naming any names. Personally check the box daily, separating letters that require your immediate attention from those that committees of students can offer solutions for. Schedule a time each week when these committees can—on Dr. King's behalf—study the facts, make objective analyses, list possible consequences, and recommend peaceful solutions.

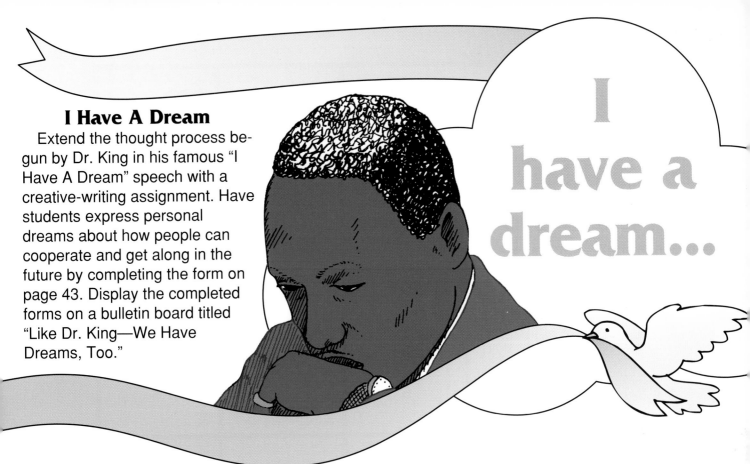

I Have A Dream

Extend the thought process begun by Dr. King in his famous "I Have A Dream" speech with a creative-writing assignment. Have students express personal dreams about how people can cooperate and get along in the future by completing the form on page 43. Display the completed forms on a bulletin board titled "Like Dr. King—We Have Dreams, Too."

Civil Rights Sites

Track the places that Dr. Martin Luther King, Jr., traveled in his pursuit of civil rights for blacks. Enlarge and mount a blank United States map on a bulletin board along with a sheet of chart paper. Throughout the study of Dr. King's efforts, keep a running list of the cities he visited on the chart paper. Have students locate them daily on the map by marking each one with a large dot or a star—to differentiate between cities and state capitals. Ask students to also add to the list other cities that they discover during independent studies. As the study progresses, lightly shade in the states Dr. King visited. Ask students to look carefully at the map, noting any areas that Dr. King visited more often than others. Have students draw conclusions about the reasons he concentrated his visits in those regions.

Montgomery, AL

Washington, DC

Selma, AL

Atlanta, GA

Chicago, IL

Detroit, MI

St. Augustine, FL

42

1. When and where was Martin Luther King, Jr., born? Describe his family.

2. Find out all you can about the kind of student Dr. King was.

3. Which college did Dr. King attend? How old was he when he enrolled? What was college life like for him?

4. What did Dr. King study in college? What did he do just before he graduated?

5. When and where did Dr. King receive his Ph.D. degree? Explain the difference between the doctoral degree he received and the one received by a medical doctor.

6. Who was Dr. King's wife? Where did they meet? What did she study?

7. How many children did Dr. King and his wife have? What were his children's names?

8. What was Dr. King's profession? Describe some of his duties.

9. Why did Dr. King move his family to Montgomery, Alabama?

10. Tell how Dr. King became involved in working for civil rights while in Montgomery, Alabama.

11. Find out why Dr. King moved from Montgomery, Alabama, to Atlanta, Georgia.

12. Describe Dr. King's speaking ability.

13. What were some of the ways people tried to discourage Dr. King and other protestors from working for civil rights?

14. Describe the March on Washington led by Dr. King and others. Tell why it was planned.

15. What was the main purpose of Dr. King's famous "I Have A Dream" speech?

16. Explain the Civil Rights Act of 1964.

17. Find out why Dr. King organized protests and marches in and near Selma, Alabama. Were they successful?

18. What were some of the conditions that Dr. King worked to improve in Chicago, Illinois?

19. What did Dr. King think of the "Black Power" movement?

20. Explain the nonviolent strategies Dr. King encouraged people to use in getting the attention of government leaders.

21. On what did Dr. King base his program of nonviolence?

22. What honor did Dr. King receive in 1964 and why?

23. Explain how Dr. King died.

24. Explain the Civil Rights Act of 1968, which was passed after Dr. King's death.

25. Dr. King's birthday is now celebrated every year as a federal holiday. How did it become a national holiday?

©1996 The Education Center, Inc. • JANUARY • TEC206

This is a reproducible to use with "Peace By Piece" on page 34. Cut apart the pieces. Then give one or more pieces to each student to research.

Note To The Teacher: Make one copy of this reproducible to use with "Peace By Piece" on page 34. Cut apart the pieces. Then give one or more pieces to each student to research.

I Have A Dream

Fill in the blanks. Then color the border.

I dream that one day I will _____

I'll help this dream come true by _____

I dream that one day my family will _____

I'll help this dream come true by _____

I dream that one day all the people in my neighborhood will _____

I'll help this dream come true by _____

I dream that one day all the people in my country will _____

I'll help this dream come true by _____

I dream that one day all the people in the world will _____

I'll help this dream come true by _____

Name _____

A Very Busy Man

Dr. Martin Luther King, Jr., lived in Montgomery, Alabama. While he was working there as a church pastor, Rosa Parks was arrested for refusing to give her bus seat to a white man. Dr. King formed a nonviolent plan that asked all black citizens to stay off the buses until unfair laws were changed. Throughout the 381 days of this bus boycott, Dr. King was a very busy man. Below is an imaginary schedule for a typical day in Dr. King's life during this historic time. Use the clues on the bus tickets to list the events in the order they occurred on his schedule.

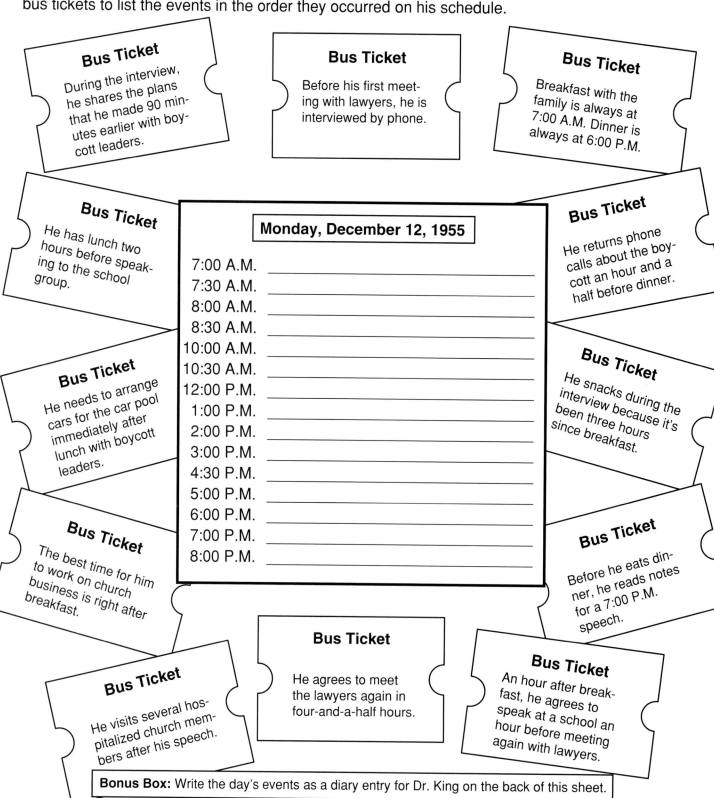

Bus Ticket
During the interview, he shares the plans that he made 90 minutes earlier with boycott leaders.

Bus Ticket
Before his first meeting with lawyers, he is interviewed by phone.

Bus Ticket
Breakfast with the family is always at 7:00 A.M. Dinner is always at 6:00 P.M.

Bus Ticket
He has lunch two hours before speaking to the school group.

Bus Ticket
He returns phone calls about the boycott an hour and a half before dinner.

Bus Ticket
He needs to arrange cars for the car pool immediately after lunch with boycott leaders.

Bus Ticket
He snacks during the interview because it's been three hours since breakfast.

Bus Ticket
The best time for him to work on church business is right after breakfast.

Bus Ticket
Before he eats dinner, he reads notes for a 7:00 P.M. speech.

Bus Ticket
He visits several hospitalized church members after his speech.

Bus Ticket
He agrees to meet the lawyers again in four-and-a-half hours.

Bus Ticket
An hour after breakfast, he agrees to speak at a school an hour before meeting again with lawyers.

Monday, December 12, 1955

7:00 A.M. _____
7:30 A.M. _____
8:00 A.M. _____
8:30 A.M. _____
10:00 A.M. _____
10:30 A.M. _____
12:00 P.M. _____
1:00 P.M. _____
2:00 P.M. _____
3:00 P.M. _____
4:30 P.M. _____
5:00 P.M. _____
6:00 P.M. _____
7:00 P.M. _____
8:00 P.M. _____

Bonus Box: Write the day's events as a diary entry for Dr. King on the back of this sheet.

What Would Dr. King Do?

Read the paragraphs about Dr. Martin Luther King, Jr., below. Then read the ten situations at the bottom of the page. What do you think Dr. King would have done in each situation? Write answers for five of the situations on the back of this paper. Support each answer with one or more facts from the paragraphs.

Dr. Martin Luther King, Jr., had an older sister and a younger brother. He was a good student. He was so smart that he skipped the 9th and 12th grades in school. He started college when he was 15 years old. Martin later received a doctorate of theology degree and became a Baptist minister.

Dr. King was an excellent speaker. He became the main leader of the civil rights movement in the United States during the 1950s and 1960s. Even after his home was bombed, he still believed that nonviolence was the way to get freedom and end discrimination. He led more than 200,000 Americans in the March on Washington. It was during this march that Dr. King made his famous "I Have A Dream" speech.

Dr. King worked to get the Voting Rights Act of 1965 passed. He also worked to increase employment opportunities, and improve bad housing and poor schools. Many times he was arrested and jailed for protesting against unfairness and discrimination. It worried him that the "Black Power" movement did not support his nonviolent ways of solving problems.

In 1964 Dr. Martin Luther King, Jr., won the Nobel Peace Prize for leading nonviolent civil rights demonstrations. Sadly, he was assassinated at the age of 39. After his death Congress passed the Civil Rights Act of 1968. This act prevented racial discrimination when persons were buying and renting most homes. Dr. King's birthday is now a federal holiday celebrated on the third Monday in January.

1.
Erin is discouraged by her low grades in school. She is thinking of dropping out.

2.
Jonathan's friends are teasing him about participating in a weekend environmental-cleanup effort at the lake.

3.
Amy doesn't believe in using animals for scientific research. She's organizing a march to say that it's wrong.

7.
Megan is concerned about a change in behavior she sees in her friends.

4.
Reggie feels neglected. His parents give his honor-roll older sister and athletic all-star brother lots of attention.

5.
B. J. is being ignored by his friends because he doesn't think the way they treat a new student is fair.

6.
Katie's friends shop at a convenience store known for its high prices. Katie refuses to buy anything there.

8.
Carrie is so angry at Kate for tattling on her that she wants to hit her at recess.

9.
Scott is determined to get a park built on a vacant lot in his neighborhood.

10.
Matt wants Brian to give their club's fund-raising speech because he has a talent for expressing himself well.

Patterns

Use with "Moved To March" on page 38.

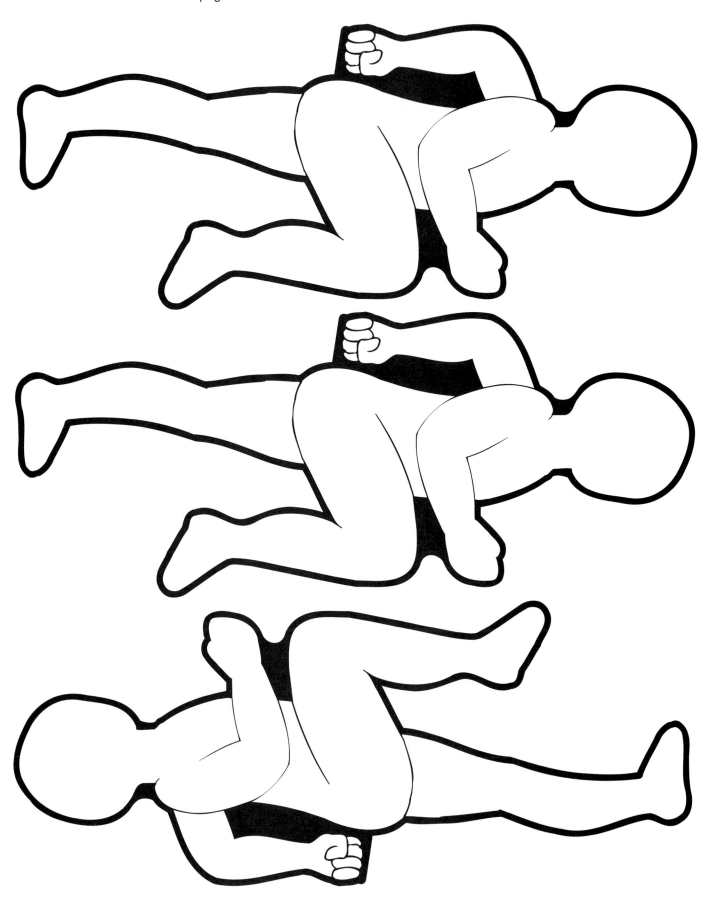

©1996 The Education Center, Inc. • *JANUARY* • TEC206

Drumming Up
The American Revolution

On January 20, 1783, British and American representatives signed a preliminary "Cessation of Hostilities," which led to the end of the American Revolution. Drum up interest in the colonists' struggle for independence with the following creative activities.

by Thad H. McLaurin and Darlene Parsons

America's First Flags

The creator of America's first flag is unknown. This is probably because flags were so popular among the colonists and many people made them. Many colonies used a smaller version of Great Britain's flag, the *Union Jack,* in the upper left corner of their flags. As the impending war with Britain loomed ahead, flags began to become more creative to express the emotions of the time. They were decorated with many different symbols including stars, stripes, and slogans. The Flag Act of June 14, 1777, declared that the American flag have a circle of 13 stars on a body of 13 red and white stripes. This flag became the official flag of the new United States. Gradually more and more stars were added as new states were formed.

Show students pictures of some of the early flag designs mentioned above (check in an encyclopedia). Then have them use the reproducible on page 54 to create their own flags. Instruct each student to cut along the dotted line above his flag after completing his design. Let each student share his flag and its symbolism; then post the flags on a bulletin board as shown (see page 59 for star patterns to add to the display).

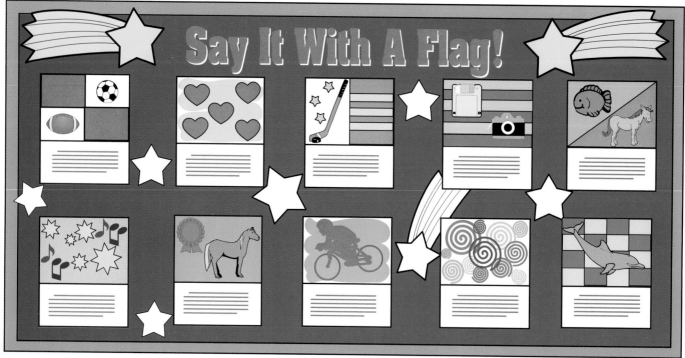

We Lost The Battle, But Won The Fight!

The Battle of Bunker Hill was one of the first battles of the American Revolution. The British went into the fight thinking the patriots would be easily defeated. In fact, the patriots suffered very few losses and only retreated when they ran out of ammunition. The British, however, suffered many casualties. The battle helped the British realize it wasn't going to be easy to defeat the Americans, and the Americans realized that they could fight the British.

Explain to students that newspapers, such as Ben Franklin's *The Pennsylvania Gazette,* were a major means of communicating news throughout the colonies. Tell students that newspapers use short, catchy headlines to grab their readers' attention. Show a few examples of headlines from your local or state newspaper. Then give each student a 5" x 17" sheet of white construction paper and a black marker. On his paper, have the student create a headline that may have appeared in a colonial newspaper the day after the Battle of Bunker Hill. Remind students that the Americans felt victorious even though they lost the battle. Let students share their headlines; then have each child write a short article to go with his headline.

A Drumroll, Please!

A drumroll, please! Announcing the Honor Roll of American Revolutionaries! A *revolutionary* may be defined as someone committed to some kind of change. The reproducible on page 55 lists 35 heroes and heroines of the American Revolution who wanted to change from being dependent colonists of Great Britain to becoming independent Americans. Have each student select one person to research. Direct students to follow the instructions on the reproducible, gather their research, and construct their cubes. Have students share their cubes with the class; then display the cubes for everyone to read.

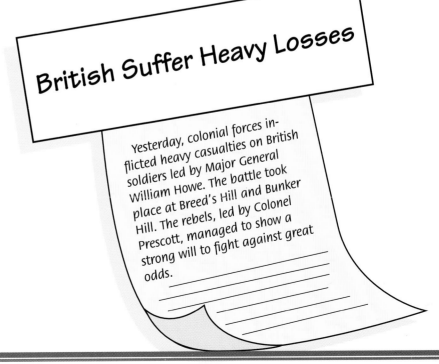

British Suffer Heavy Losses

Yesterday, colonial forces inflicted heavy casualties on British soldiers led by Major General William Howe. The battle took place at Breed's Hill and Bunker Hill. The rebels, led by Colonel Prescott, managed to show a strong will to fight against great odds.

A Message To George

The Declaration Of Independence is a powerful document in which Thomas Jefferson clearly stated the feelings of the American patriots. Jefferson spent 17 days carefully choosing his words for the document. He divided the document into four sections—Introduction, Beliefs, Wrongs, and Conclusion. Each section clearly sent a message to King George.

Divide students into pairs. Give each pair a copy of the reproducible on page 56 and a copy of the Declaration Of Independence. Instruct students to read each section of the document, then use the reproducible to paraphrase each section. (Students may need dictionaries to look up unfamiliar words.) After students have completed the activity, have various pairs share their interpretations of the Declaration Of Independence. Finally have students share their responses to the three questions at the bottom of the reproducible.

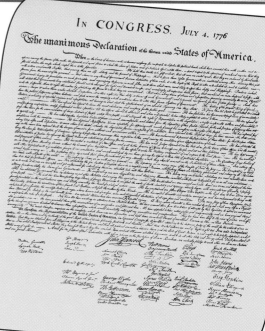

We Have Rights, Too!

The colonists felt they had no rights under British control. Students sometimes feel that they have no rights because they are still "kids." Help your students realize their rights as young people. Divide your students into groups and give each group two pieces of poster board and a marker. Tell each group to brainstorm a list of rights for kids and write it on one piece of poster board. Instruct the students to fill the other piece of poster board with catchy slogans that express the rights they've listed. Have each group share its slogans; then post the posters around the room.

Next let the students express their rights by creating T-shirts decorated with the slogans they've created. Ask each student to bring in a prewashed, white T-shirt. Supply students with fabric paints, fabric markers, and brushes. Insert a piece of cardboard inside each T-shirt to prevent the paints and markers from bleeding. Tell each student to lightly trace a slogan on her T-shirt with a pencil before painting. Finally have a "Kids' Rights Day" on which everyone wears his T-shirt.

Women And The War

Women could not fight in the Revolutionary War, but they did band together to support the cause of liberty. They boycotted English goods and took over the businesses and farms when the men left to fight. Deborah Sampson even disguised herself as a man and fought undetected for nearly two years, while Deborah Champion served as a spy for General Washington. Some women even helped load cannons.

Have students brainstorm a list of reasons why they think women were not allowed to fight in the Revolutionary War. Then ask students: "How have women's roles changed since the Revolutionary War? What is your opinion about women fighting in a war?" Next instruct each student to write an essay about women fighting in active combat. Tell students to state their opinions and give details to support them. Let students share their essays; then discuss the various opinions.

Suggest the following books to students who would like to read more about women during the Revolutionary War:

- *Sybil Rides For Independence* by Drollene Brown (Albert Whitman & Co., 1985)
- *This Time, Tempe Wick?* by Patricia L. Gauch (The Putnam Publishing Group, 1992)
- *Who Is Carrie?* by James L. Collier and Christopher Collier (Dell Publishing Co., Inc.; 1987)

From Lexington To Yorktown

From Lexington and Concord to Yorktown, major battles play an important part in understanding the sequence of events of the American Revolution. Divide the class into five groups. Give a copy of page 57 to each group. Assign each group one of the following battles: Lexington and Concord, Bunker Hill, Trenton, Saratoga, and Yorktown. Provide the class with a variety of reference materials. After the groups have completed their research and filled out their copies of page 57, post a U.S. map or a map of the 13 colonies in the classroom. Let each group share information about its battle; then have the group tack its completed reproducible around the edge of the map. Connect the reproducible to the location of the battle with yarn and pushpins. Finally have students decide the order of the battles by numbering the reproducibles 1–5. Students can now easily see the order of events that occurred during the Revolution.

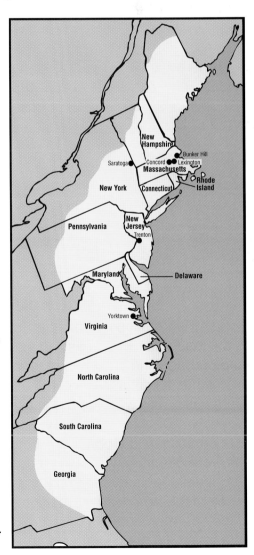

African-Americans And The War

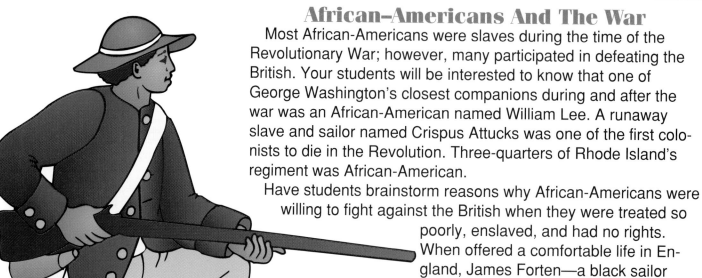

Most African-Americans were slaves during the time of the Revolutionary War; however, many participated in defeating the British. Your students will be interested to know that one of George Washington's closest companions during and after the war was an African-American named William Lee. A runaway slave and sailor named Crispus Attucks was one of the first colonists to die in the Revolution. Three-quarters of Rhode Island's regiment was African-American.

Have students brainstorm reasons why African-Americans were willing to fight against the British when they were treated so poorly, enslaved, and had no rights. When offered a comfortable life in England, James Forten—a black sailor from Pennsylvania—said, "No, I'm a prisoner for my country, and I'll never be a traitor to her." Share this quote with students. Then have each student write a journal entry that Crispus Attucks or James Forten might have written explaining why he felt it was his duty to join in the fight against Britain.

Spies And Secret Messages

Spies were used by both the British and Americans. James Armistead (later known as James Lafayette) was a black slave and probably the most important of the American spies. He worked as a waiter in the camp of a British general, Lord Cornwallis, and was instrumental in the capture of Cornwallis at Yorktown. Deborah Champion and Lydia Darragh helped relay secret messages to George Washington. Secret codes and invisible ink were often used in case messages were intercepted.

Have students try their hands at breaking a secret code used by a spy of the American Revolution. Give each student a copy of page 58. After students have broken the spy code and the code of a friend, let them share whether the codes were easy or difficult to break.

General Howe:
STRIKE
Be advised that we
AT
make every effort
DAWN!
assist you. You may
messenger
implicitly.

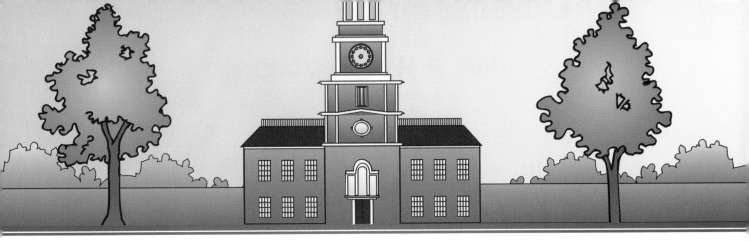

Call It Macaroni?

The beloved song "Yankee Doodle" was originally sung by British soldiers to ridicule the patriots. Americans, however, liked the tune and began singing it in their camps and during battle. Many have wondered what *macaroni* refers to in the song. Macaroni was a slang expression for a *dandy* or *fashionable* gentleman. The British wore very elaborate uniforms and made fun of the Americans, who fought in work clothes. For more information, read *Yankee Doodle* by Gary Chalk (Dorling Kindersley, Inc.; 1993).

Divide students into small groups. Have each group write a new verse for "Yankee Doodle" that describes a particular event of the American Revolution (the Boston Tea Party, Lexington and Concord, etc.). Encourage students to use current and appropriate slang words in their verses. Type a copy of the students' verses in chronological order; then have the class perform its new rendition of "Yankee Doodle" for other classes in your grade level.

Jean Fritz To The Rescue!

Are some of your students just not interested in learning about the Revolutionary War? Maybe it's the uninviting way facts and figures are presented in history books. Jean Fritz has written a series of books that are perfect for both avid and reluctant historians. Instead of compiling all of the events of the American Revolution into one huge book, Fritz has broken it up into a series of titles like *What's The Big Idea, Ben Franklin?; And Then What Happened, Paul Revere?; Will You Sign Here, John Hancock?;* and *Why Don't You Get A Horse, Sam Adams?* (Scholastic Inc.). Each short book includes captivating illustrations to intrigue young readers. Incorporate Fritz's books into your classroom with these ideas:

- Share all or selected books with the class as read-alouds.
- Have students read the books independently and give book-talk presentations.
- Divide the class into small groups; then assign a different book to each group.
- Make a listening center by tape-recording the books on cassettes.
- Have the books available for research.

Say It With A Flag!

A flag is a symbol for an important idea, value, or event. For the American colonists, flags represented independence and liberty. Using the following steps, create your own flag in the space below.

Step 1: Think of something important to you that you want to express in a flag. It can represent an event, a problem, a group of people, a celebration, etc.

Step 2: Decide on the colors and symbols that would be good to use on your flag.

Step 3: Decide if a slogan is needed. Remember to keep it short and simple.

Step 4: Using a pencil, sketch your flag in the box.

Step 5: Use crayons, markers, or colored pencils to color your flag.

Step 6: After completing your flag, write a brief description of it and its purpose in the space at the bottom of the page.

Description And Purpose: _____

_____

_____

_____

Note To The Teacher: Use with "America's First Flags" on page 48. Make one copy for each student. Provide 54 students with scissors and crayons, markers, or colored pencils.

American Revolutionaries

Directions:

1. Choose one revolutionary from the list at the right to research.
2. Fill in the information on the diagram.
3. Put an original illustration related to the person in the box labeled "Illustration."
4. Cut very carefully along the solid lines only.
5. Fold along the dotted lines to form a cube. (The writing should be on the outside of the cube.)
6. Glue the tabs to the inside of the cube.

I believe he/she should be honored because...

Name List

Abigail Adams
John Adams
Samuel Adams
James Armistead (Lafayette)
Crispus Attucks
Deborah Champion
Oliver Cromwell
Lydia Darragh
William Dawes
John Dickinson
James Forten
Benjamin Franklin
Mary Katharine Goddard
Nathanael Greene
John Hancock
Patrick Henry
Thomas Jefferson
John Paul Jones
Henry Knox
Richard Henry Lee
William Lee
Robert Livingston
Sybil Ludington
Francis Marion
Thomas Paine
John Parker
Molly Pitcher (Mary Ludwig)
Samuel Prescott
Paul Revere
Peter Salem
Deborah Sampson
Roger Sherman
Joseph Warren
George Washington
Sarah Wister

Early Life

I believe he/she should be honored because…

Illustration

Contributions To The War

Name Of The Revolutionary

TAB

TAB

TAB

Early Life

Career(s) Pursued

TAB

TAB

TAB

Note To The Teacher: Use this reproducible with "A Drumroll, Please!" on page 49. Provide each student with one copy of the reproducible, scissors, glue, and crayons, markers, or colored pencils.

Names:_____ *Writing: paraphrasing*

The Declaration Of Independence

Thomas Jefferson divided the Declaration Of Independence into four main parts. Using a copy of the Declaration Of Independence and a dictionary, work with your partner to write each part in your own words. Try to keep the same meaning but use words and phrases of today. Then answer the questions about the document below.

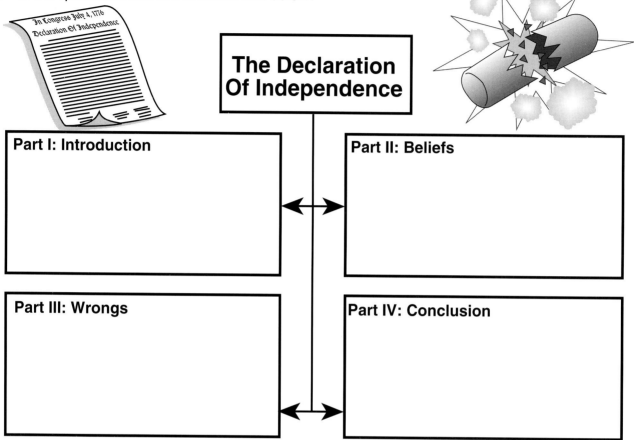

The Declaration Of Independence

Part I: Introduction

Part II: Beliefs

Part III: Wrongs

Part IV: Conclusion

Questions:

1. What was the purpose of the document?_____
   _____
   _____
   _____

2. Colonel John Nixon read the Declaration Of Independence from a platform at Carpenters' Hall in Philadelphia on July 8, 1776. How do you think the colonists felt when they heard him?_____
   _____
   _____
   _____

3. How do you think King George III of Great Britain felt when he received the Declaration Of Independence?_____
   _____
   _____

Bonus Box: On the back, draw a cartoon illustration of King George III receiving the Declaration Of Independence. Write a humorous caption telling what he may have said when he received the document.

©1996 The Education Center, Inc. • *JANUARY* • TEC206

Note To The Teacher: Use with "A Message To George" on page 50. See page 95 for a brief paraphrase of each section.

Group Members

Battles Of The Revolution

Write the name of the Revolutionary War battle assigned to your group in the box below.
Use reference materials to find details for each subtopic of your battle.

_____
(Name Of Battle)

Time & Place	Cause or Purpose	Battle Strategies	Morale of Troops	Results
Details	Details	Details	Details	Details

Bonus Box: What if this battle had not turned out as it did? What if the other side had won? How would it have changed the outcome of the war? Write your responses to these questions on the back.

Note To The Teacher: Use with "From Lexington To Yorktown" on page 51. Divide the class into five groups. Make one copy of this page for each group. Assign each group a different battle to research. Suggested battles include Lexington and Concord, Bunker Hill, Trenton, Saratoga, and Yorktown.

Break The Code

Many spies of the American Revolution used secret codes when writing messages. Some spies wrote in foreign languages, others left out letters, and some even used invisible ink. Below is a familiar message about the Revolution that is written in a code actually used by an American spy for the British. Write the message on the lines provided.

Hint: A=Z, B=Y, etc.

"Orhgvm, nb xsrowivm, zmw blf hszoo svzi
Lu gsv nrwmrtsg irwv lu Kzfo Iveviv,
Lm gsv vrtsgvvmgs lu Zkiro, rm Hvevmgb-urev;
Sziwob z nzm rh mld zorev
Dsl ivnvnyvih gszg uznlfh wzb zmw bvzi."
        —yb Svmib Dzwhdligs Olmtuvoold

_____
_____
_____
_____
_____

Now it's your turn. Use letters, numbers, or symbols to create your own code on another piece of paper. Write a secret message on the lines below. Pass your message to a friend and see if he or she can break it.

_____
_____
_____
_____
_____
_____
_____
_____
_____
_____
_____
_____

Bonus Box: Some spies just left out letters in a word to make it difficult to read. Write a secret message on another piece of paper using this method. Give it to a friend to try to decode.

©1996 The Education Center, Inc. • *JANUARY* • TEC206 • Key p. 95

58 **Note To The Teacher:** Use with "Spies And Secret Messages" on page 52.

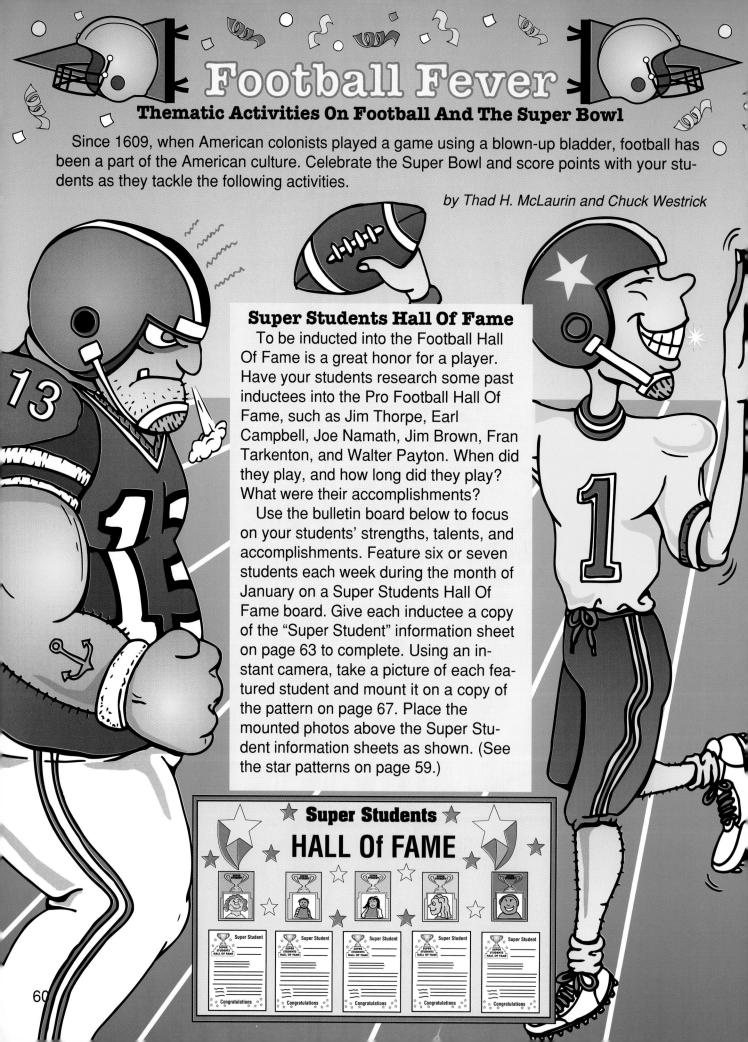

Football Fever
Thematic Activities On Football And The Super Bowl

Since 1609, when American colonists played a game using a blown-up bladder, football has been a part of the American culture. Celebrate the Super Bowl and score points with your students as they tackle the following activities.

by Thad H. McLaurin and Chuck Westrick

Super Students Hall Of Fame

To be inducted into the Football Hall Of Fame is a great honor for a player. Have your students research some past inductees into the Pro Football Hall Of Fame, such as Jim Thorpe, Earl Campbell, Joe Namath, Jim Brown, Fran Tarkenton, and Walter Payton. When did they play, and how long did they play? What were their accomplishments?

Use the bulletin board below to focus on your students' strengths, talents, and accomplishments. Feature six or seven students each week during the month of January on a Super Students Hall Of Fame board. Give each inductee a copy of the "Super Student" information sheet on page 63 to complete. Using an instant camera, take a picture of each featured student and mount it on a copy of the pattern on page 67. Place the mounted photos above the Super Student information sheets as shown. (See the star patterns on page 59.)

★ **Super Students** ★
HALL Of FAME

Super Student

Congratulations

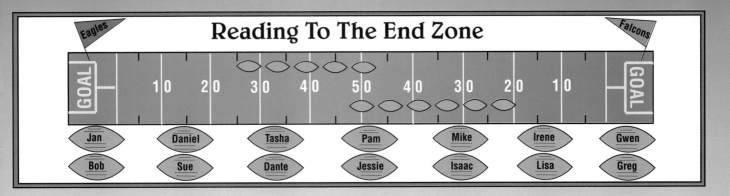

Reading To The End Zone

Eagles Falcons

GOAL 10 20 30 40 50 40 30 20 10 GOAL

Jan Daniel Tasha Pam Mike Irene Gwen

Bob Sue Dante Jessie Isaac Lisa Greg

Reading To The End Zone

Increase your students' interest in reading during the month of January with this exciting and fun reading contest. Divide the class into two teams. Instruct each team to select a team name to use during the contest. Create a football field by cutting a six-foot piece of green bulletin-board paper. Divide the paper into six-inch sections. Label the first six inches and last six inches as goals. Divided the remaining six-inch sections into three-inch sections; then mark every ten yards as shown. Place team pennants at each goal. Post the paper in the hall or on a classroom bulletin board. Make copies of the football reproducible on page 64. As each student reads a book, have her complete the football reproducible, then tape it under the field. Next write the student's name on a small football marker (page 67); then place it on the next yard line for her team—starting at the 50-yard line and moving in five-yard increments toward her team's goal. The first team to reach its goal line wins the contest.

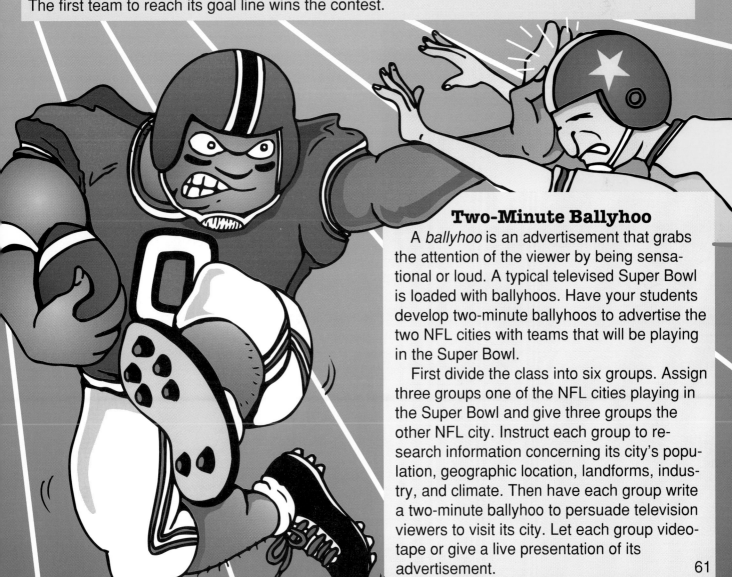

Two-Minute Ballyhoo

A *ballyhoo* is an advertisement that grabs the attention of the viewer by being sensational or loud. A typical televised Super Bowl is loaded with ballyhoos. Have your students develop two-minute ballyhoos to advertise the two NFL cities with teams that will be playing in the Super Bowl.

First divide the class into six groups. Assign three groups one of the NFL cities playing in the Super Bowl and give three groups the other NFL city. Instruct each group to research information concerning its city's population, geographic location, landforms, industry, and climate. Then have each group write a two-minute ballyhoo to persuade television viewers to visit its city. Let each group videotape or give a live presentation of its advertisement.

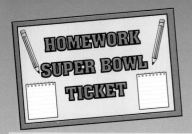

Homework Super Bowl Tickets

Give away your own version of Super Bowl tickets as an incentive for completing daily assignments in January. Inform the students that beginning on the first school day in January, they will each be able to earn one Homework Super Bowl ticket for every day that they complete all required assignments. Tell the class that they will be able to redeem their tickets for various prizes at a Homework Super Bowl party on the last Friday of January.

Make several copies of the ticket patterns on page 67. At the end of each day, give one ticket to each child who has completed all his assignments. Before the party, ask parent volunteers to provide small prizes and a variety of individually wrapped goodies. You can also offer prizes such as coupons for computer time or homework passes. Ask parent volunteers to manage the trading of tickets for prizes and goodies at the party. While the trading is going on, set up a special movie—perhaps with a football theme—for students to view.

Super Bowl Quiz Game

Celebrate the upcoming Super Bowl showdown with the following review game. Divide the class into two teams. Draw a football field on the board, marking every ten yards. Write the name of each team at a goal line. Place a piece of tape on the back of one of the small footballs on page 67. On index cards, have students write questions reviewing skills and concepts taught earlier in the year. Instruct students to write the answers on the backs of the cards. For fun, throw in a few trivia questions about the real Super Bowl.

To begin play, place the football marker on the 50-yard line; then flip a coin to see which team goes first. Ask Team One a question. If it answers correctly, move the football ten yards in the direction of that team's goal; then ask the team another question. If the team answers incorrectly, Team Two gains control of the ball. If Team Two answers correctly, move the ball ten yards in the direction of its goal. Trivia questions are worth five yards, but do not penalize teams if they answer these questions incorrectly. Once a touchdown is made, return the ball to the 50-yard line and resume the game.

Super Student

_____
(Name)

_____
(Date)

_____
(Address)

Family: _____

Three Words That Best Describe Me: _____, _____, and_____

Favorite Book: _____

Favorite School Subject: _____

Favorite Food: _____

Favorite Restaurant: _____

Favorite Singer/Musical Group: _____

Favorite Movie: _____

Something That Makes Me Proud: _____

Things I'm Good At Doing: _____

One Wish I Have: _____

Career Goals: _____

Congratulations!

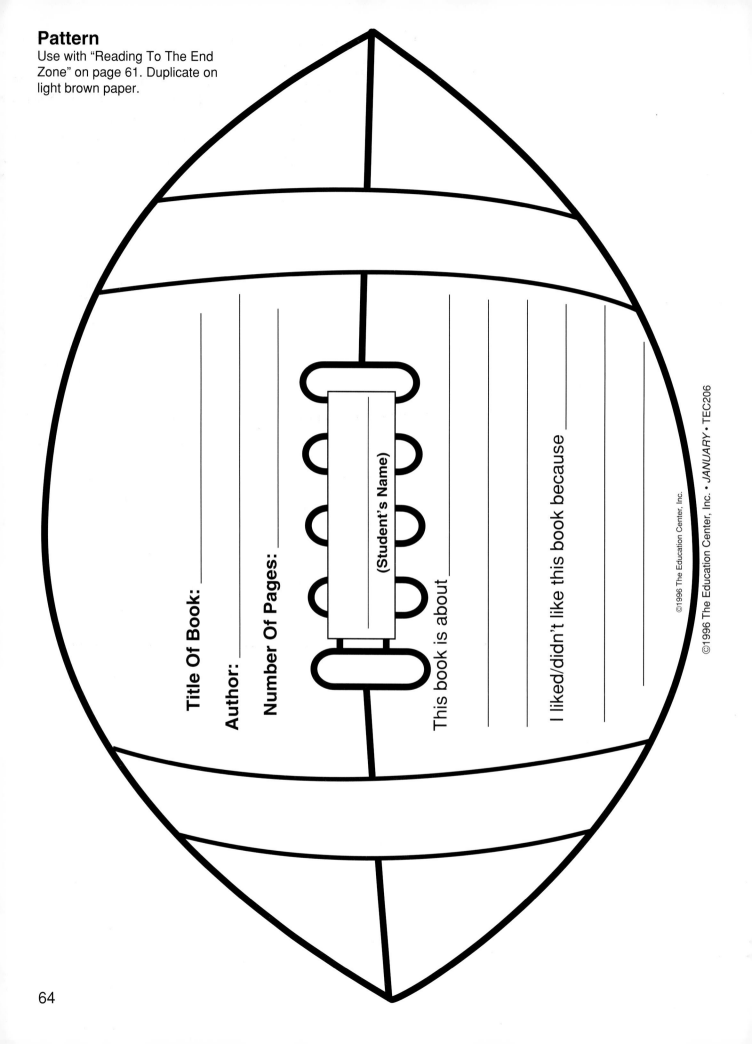

Pattern
Use with "Reading To The End Zone" on page 61. Duplicate on light brown paper.

Title Of Book: _____

Author: _____

Number Of Pages: _____

(Student's Name)

This book is about _____

I liked/didn't like this book because _____

©1996 The Education Center, Inc. • JANUARY • TEC206

©1996 The Education Center, Inc.

64

Go For The Goal!

Young football players around the world dream of making it *big* one day in professional football. No matter what you dream of doing in the future, setting goals for yourself can help you be successful. After careful thinking, fill in one, two, three, or four long-range goals for yourself. Then decide on the short-range, weekly, and daily goals you will need to meet in order to achieve your long-range goals. Post this sheet where you will see it frequently to help remind you of your goals.

LONG-RANGE GOALS

1. _____
2. _____
3. _____
4. _____

SHORT-RANGE GOALS

1. _____
2. _____
3. _____
4. _____

WEEKLY GOALS

1. _____
2. _____
3. _____
4. _____

DAILY GOALS

1. _____
2. _____
3. _____
4. _____

Bonus Box: On the back of this sheet, write a paragraph about a career goal you have for the future. What would you like to be? What do you think you'll need to do to help you reach this goal?

Note To The Teacher: To help students better understand short- and long-range goals, explain that for them short-range goals are ones that can be achieved in three to four weeks, while long-range goals can be achieved in a six- or nine-week grading period.

Name _____

Estimation Concession Session

Use the menu board and your estimation skills to determine if the sports fans below have enough money to make their purchases. Estimate the total for each problem by rounding to the nearest dollar. Then use a calculator to find the exact total. Determine how much change the sports fans will receive or how much more money they need to make their purchases. Underline "Change Due" or "Money Needed"; then fill in the amount.

★ ★ ★ ★ ★ ★ ★ ★ ★ ★ ★ ★ ★ ★ ★ **Concession Stand** ★ ★ ★ ★ ★ ★ ★ ★ ★ ★ ★ ★ ★ ★ ★

Touchdown Tortilla $1.59	Halftime Hot Dog .... $.99	Locker-Room Lollipop .... $.65
First-Down Fajita $2.39	Stadium Burger $2.19	Large Drink $1.00
Tight-End Taco $1.39	Field-Goal Fries .... $.69	Medium Drink .... $.75
Big Band Burrito $1.99	Punter's Popcorn $1.25	Small Drink .... $.50
Coach's Corn Dog .... $.89	Cheerleader's Candy .... $.50	Program $3.00

---

1. Toby and Carlos have $15.00. They want to order two Big Band Burritos and three First-Down Fajitas plus a program.
   Estimate: _____ Exact Total: _____ Change Due or Money Needed: _____

2. Ned's friends sent him to the concession stand with $10.00. They told him to buy three Punter's Popcorns, one Stadium Burger, and five medium drinks.
   Estimate: _____ Exact Total: _____ Change Due or Money Needed: _____

3. Alex loves corn dogs! He has $5.00 and wants to order four Coach's Corn Dogs, one Field-Goal Fries, and a large drink.
   Estimate: _____ Exact Total: _____ Change Due or Money Needed: _____

4. Fifteen fans sitting on the 50-yard line each want a small drink. They collect a total of $9.25.
   Estimate: _____ Exact Total: _____ Change Due or Money Needed: _____

5. The members of Danielle's family decide they each want two Touchdown Tortillas, one Locker-Room Lollipop, and one medium drink. There are four people in her family. Her parents give her a twenty-dollar bill.
   Estimate: _____ Exact Total: _____ Change Due or Money Needed: _____

6. Arlene brought $15.00 to the game. She wants to buy lunch for her friends. Arlene orders four Halftime Hot Dogs, two Tight-End Tacos, four Field-Goal Fries, one large drink, two medium drinks, one small drink, and four Cheerleader's Candies.
   Estimate: _____ Exact Total: _____ Change Due or Money Needed: _____

7. Andy and Bob are starving at halftime. They each order one First-Down Fajita, one Touchdown Tortilla, one Field-Goal Fries, and one large drink. They have $10.00 to spend together.
   Estimate: _____ Exact Total: _____ Change Due or Money Needed: _____

8. Sarita has $3.00 and Rhonda has $1.75. Together they order two Punter's Popcorns, one Cheerleader's Candy, one Locker-Room Lollipop, and two medium drinks.
   Estimate: _____ Exact Total: _____ Change Due or Money Needed: _____

9. Meg's really hungry. She orders two Stadium Burgers, two Field-Goal Fries, and one large drink. She has $8.00 in her pocket.
   Estimate: _____ Exact Total: _____ Change Due or Money Needed: _____

10. Gwen wants to surprise her friend. She sneaks to the concession stand and orders two Halftime Hot Dogs, one Punter's Popcorn, and two small drinks. Gwen has $4.75.
    Estimate: _____ Exact Total: _____ Change Due or Money Needed: _____

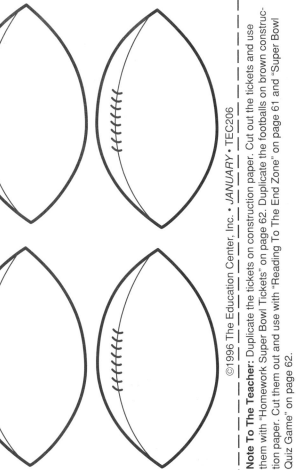

HOMEWORK SUPER BOWL TICKET

HOMEWORK SUPER BOWL TICKET

HOMEWORK SUPER BOWL TICKET

HOMEWORK SUPER BOWL TICKET

©1996 The Education Center, Inc. • *JANUARY* • TEC206

Note To The Teacher: Duplicate the tickets on construction paper. Cut out the tickets and use them with "Homework Super Bowl Tickets" on page 62. Duplicate the footballs on brown construction paper. Cut them out and use with "Reading To The End Zone" on page 61 and "Super Bowl Quiz Game" on page 62.

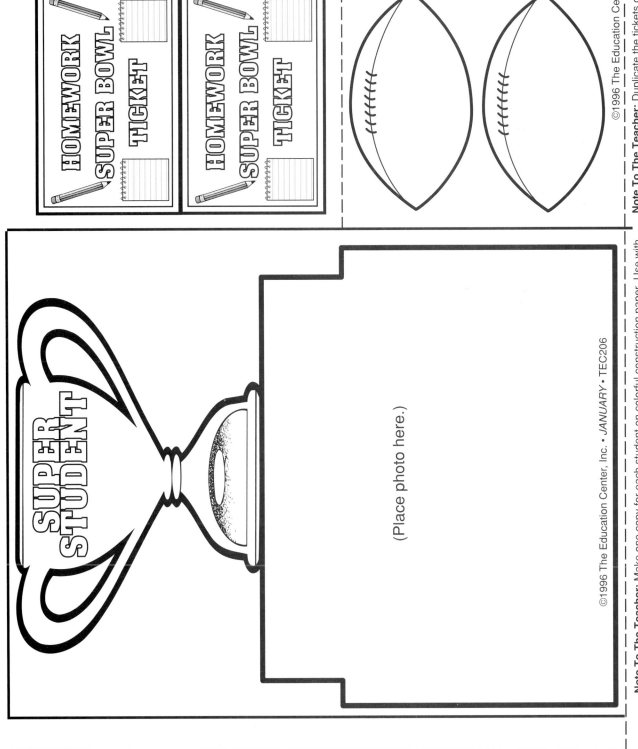

SUPER STUDENT

(Place photo here.)

©1996 The Education Center, Inc. • *JANUARY* • TEC206

Note To The Teacher: Make one copy for each student on colorful construction paper. Use with "Super Students Hall Of Fame" on page 60.

Searching The Friendly Skies

Out-Of-This-World Activities For Studying Space

Three…two…one…blast off into a new year with some truly far-out space activities! The month of January has a payload of space history milestones (see the chart below). What better time than now to propel your students into a thematic study of space, the final frontier?

by Patricia Twohey

Extraterrestrial Terminology

Help your students latch on to space vocabulary with easy-to-make flash cards. Duplicate the vocabulary list on page 78. Cut out each word/definition strip and wrap it around a 4" x 6" index card as shown. Use the resulting flash cards in the following ways:

- Place the cards at a learning center for students to use when quizzing each other.
- Shuffle the cards and give one to each student. Instruct each student to act out the term without speaking. Have other class members try to guess the word.
- Divide the class into two teams. In turn, have a member from each team come to the board. Call out a definition. Have each student write the correct term on the board. Award teams a point for the correct answer and an extra point for correct spelling.
- Duplicate page 78 for each student to use for making his own card set.

space shuttle

A reusable spacecraft controlled or piloted by astronauts

Space Milestones In January

Date	Milestone
Jan. 31, 1958	*Explorer I,* the first successful U.S. satellite, was launched. It transmitted signals until May 23, 1958, and discovered the Van Allen Belt.
Jan. 2, 1959	*Luna 1* (USSR) became the first spacecraft from Earth to orbit the sun.
Jan. 31, 1961	A Mercury capsule was launched carrying Ham, the chimpanzee. Ham successfully transmitted signals and was returned safely to Earth.
Jan. 31, 1966	*Luna 9* (USSR) was launched and later conducted the first soft landing on the moon. The unmanned ship sent photos back to Earth.
Jan. 27, 1967	Fire broke out on *Apollo I* (USA) during a launching simulation test, killing three astronauts.
Jan. 14, 1969	*Soyuz 4* (USSR) launches and docks with another manned spacecraft and conducts the first interchange of spaceship personnel in orbit.
Jan. 31, 1971	*Apollo 14* (USA) was launched and later landed on the moon.
Jan. 16, 1973	*Luna 21* (USSR), an unmanned vehicle, landed on the moon carrying a radio-controlled vehicle that explored its surface.
Jan. 10, 1975	*Soyuz 17* (USSR) was launched carrying two cosmonauts who spent 28 of their 30 days in the space station *Salyut 4.*
Jan. 10, 1978	*Soyuz 27* (USSR), carrying two cosmonauts, was launched and linked with the *Salyut 6* space station.
Jan. 24–27, 1985	The space shuttle *Discovery* (USA) conducted a secret, all-military mission to deploy an eavesdropping satellite.
Jan. 28, 1986	The space shuttle *Challenger* (USA) exploded shortly after takeoff, killing seven crew members including school teacher Christa McAuliffe.

Gravity—A Weighty Matter

Use this appealing demonstration to get your students thinking about *gravitation*—the mysterious glue that holds the universe together. Bring in three 10-pound bags of apples, three plastic grocery bags, a kitchen scale, and a bathroom scale. Before students arrive, open two of the bags of apples and measure 3.8 pounds, 9 pounds, and 1.6 pounds of apples, placing each amount in a separate grocery bag. Then duplicate page 79 for each student and follow these steps:

1. Explain that *weight* is the force of *gravity* on the mass of an object. Since each planet has a different *mass,* the force of gravity is not the same on every planet. Therefore a bag of apples will not weigh the same on each planet.
2. Have a student hold the 10-pound bag of apples in one hand and the 3.8-pound bag in the other; then have him compare the weights. Explain that gravity on Mercury is about a third of what it is on Earth. Therefore a 10-pound bag of apples would actually weigh only 3.8 pounds on Mercury. Have students notice this statistic in column 3 of the chart on page 79. Have students also notice that one Earth-pound is equal to only 0.38 pounds on Mercury (column 2).
3. Repeat step 2 using the 9-pound bag, looking at the information on the chart for Venus. *(A bag of apples that weighs 10 pounds on Earth weighs only 9 pounds on Venus.)* Then repeat step 2 using the 1.6-pound bag, studying the chart's information on the moon. *(A bag of apples that weighs 10 pounds on Earth would weigh only 1.6 pounds on the moon.)*
4. After looking at the info for Mercury, Venus, and the moon, ask students if they notice any pattern in the relationship between the numbers in column 2 and in column 3 (the decimal in column 2 is moved to the right one digit in column 3). After pointing out the pattern, have each student complete column 3 of the chart.
5. Finish by having each student weigh himself on the bathroom scale. Instruct the student to follow the directions on page 79 to discover how much he would weigh on each planet and the moon. Have the student fill in this information in column 4 of his chart.

10 lb.   9 lb.

Captain's Log

Organize your space unit by having each student create a captain's log to keep track of the completed activities. Have each student bring in an empty cereal box. Instruct the student to cut off the top flaps, then cover the box with colorful paper. Next give each child a copy of the label patterns on page 77. Instruct the student to color and personalize the large astronaut pattern, then paste it onto the front of his box. Have the student color each of the other labels and save them in the box. With the completion of each activity, have the student select a label, fill in the name of the space activity and the date on which it was completed, cut it out, and paste it onto the front of his box. Any written work can be stored in the box for the teacher to look at later. Post the boxes on a bulletin board labeled "Mission Control" or on a bookshelf.

Activity: Gravity Experiment

Date: Jan. 13

Activity: Moon Art Project

Date: Jan. 9

Josh Teal
Student Name
ASTRONAUT

All In One Year

Many characteristics of the Earth can be explained using a model. Place a brightly colored Post-It™ Brand note on a globe to mark your state's location. Point out that the Earth tilts about 23.5° on its axis. Have a student stand in the center of the class holding a lit flashlight to represent the sun. Have another child hold the globe tilted at an angle. Instruct the Earth student to walk in a counterclockwise orbit around the sun, turning the globe in a counterclockwise direction as he walks (to represent the passing of days). Instruct the sun to shine its light on the globe as the Earth student circles her. Point out that it takes 365 days (one year) to complete this orbit. Discuss the effect this movement has on the length of the Earth's seasons.

Next ask students, "Would you be the same age if you lived on another planet in our solar system?" Help students find the answer by having them complete copies of page 81.

Seeing Is Believing

Help students visualize the huge orbits of the planets around the sun with the following model. Duplicate page 80 for each student. After completing the chart on the page, assign each of nine groups a planet. Give each group a pair of scissors, a 9" x 12" sheet of colored paper, a ruler, and a colored marker. In addition you will need a supply of yarn. Instruct each group to label its paper with the name of the group's planet. Then have the group cut a length of yarn equal to the measurement figured on the fourth column of the chart on page 80.

Next have each group carry its yarn and label out to the playground or to the gym. Place a large yellow circle in the center of the area and have a volunteer stand on it to represent the sun. Beginning with Mercury, have a member from each planet's group hold an end of the yarn length in one hand and the planet label in the other hand; then have him give the other end of the yarn to the sun to hold. Because the planets Mercury, Venus, and Earth are relatively close together, the students representing these planets will have to stand close together. Once the student-sun is holding the end of each planet's yarn, instruct all of the planets to move slowly in a counterclockwise circle around the sun. Direct each planet to move carefully—using the yarn length as a guide—in order to maintain the correct distance from the sun. As each student-planet moves around the sun, explain that the actual orbit of each planet is elliptical, not circular, in shape. Point out that this model simply shows students the relative distance and size of each planet's orbit.

Satellite Savvy

Take a closer look at the members of our solar system with this investigative activity. Divide the class into nine groups. Randomly assign one planet to each group to research. Duplicate two copies of page 82 for each group. Give the group one copy to use as a guide during its research. Have the group complete another copy to display. After each group has cut out the three pieces on its completed sheet and glued them together as shown below, post the resulting satellites on a bulletin board titled "Satellite Savvy." Then give each group five index cards. Instruct each group to use its research to devise five riddles—writing the riddle on one side of each card and the name of the planet on the opposite side. Gather the cards from each group, shuffle them, and store them in a pocket on the bulletin board. Invite students to quiz each other during free time.

Moonstruck

Scientists have identified over 60 moons in our galaxy. Listed to the right are the names of the larger, better-known moons (excluding ours). Duplicate 28 copies of the moon pattern on page 83. Copy the name of each moon onto a separate pattern. Pin these on a bulletin board titled "Moonstruck." Challenge each student to research one or more moons. Then have him write a short fact on the front or back of the corresponding pattern along with his initials. Reward each student with one point for each fact.

As an alternative, pass the completed moon patterns to the nine groups used in the "Satellite Savvy" idea above. Have each group write one or more riddles for the moons on index cards. Then add the moon patterns and riddles to the "Satellite Savvy" board.

Moons

Ananke	Leda
Ariel	Lysithea
Callisto	Mimas
Carme	Miranda
Charon	Nereid
Deimos	Oberon
Dione	Pasiphae
Elara	Phobos
Enceladus	Phoebe
Europa	Rhea
Ganymede	Sinope
Himalia	Tethys
Hyperion	Titan
Io	Triton

Postcards From Space

Here's a far-out way to share space research with fellow classmates! Have each student imagine that she is on vacation in space (for instance, soaking up solar rays on Venus, roping a rocky ride on an asteroid, or spelunking on a cavernous moon). Have her research the location and imagine what it would be like to vacation there. Then have her write a postcard to a friend expressing her feelings and insights about this particular vacation. Give each student a 9" x 6" sheet of heavy white paper on which to write her message and the address of the recipient. Instruct her to add a stamp and a postmark for an authentic look. Then have her flip over the card and add an illustration of her intergalactic destination.

Dear Mike,
This planet is really great! Jupiter is so big that I won't have time to see the other side. Our hotel is a giant, floating space station. Yesterday we parachuted through the clouds. It was spooky not seeing where we were landing. Later we took a shuttle ride over the Great Red Spot—awesome! See you soon with more news!

Pat

Mike Joseph
320 Appletree Lane
Ciderville, RI 02020
U.S.A.
Earth

Space Pioneers

Introduce your students to the first men and women of space by copying the names of space pioneers below on slips of paper. Have each student draw one name to determine the space pioneer he will research. Duplicate the astronaut pattern on page 83 for each student. Instruct each student to use the *who, what, when, where,* and *why* categories on his pattern to guide his research. After completing the information on the pattern, have each student attach it to a bulletin board. Cut out a simple spaceship outline and label it "Space Pioneers"; then color the spaceship and mount it on the bulletin board. Attach each of the completed astronauts to the spaceship with a tether of colorful yarn.

Nicolaus Copernicus
Isaac Newton
Konstantin Tsiolkovsky
Clyde Tombaugh
Alan B. Shepard, Jr.
Alexei Leonov
Edwin E. Aldrin, Jr.
Sally K. Ride
Bruce McCandless
Christa McAuliffe
Eileen M. Collins

Johannes Kepler
Edmond Halley
Edwin P. Hubble
Wernher von Braun
John H. Glenn, Jr.
Edward H. White II
Michael Collins
Guion S. Bluford
Marc Garneau
Norman Thagard
Galileo Galilei

William Herschel
Robert H. Goddard
Yuri A. Gagarin
Valentina Tereshkova
Neil A. Armstrong
James A. Lovell, Jr.
Svetlana Savitskaya
Kathryn D. Sullivan
Mae C. Jemison
Shannon W. Lucid

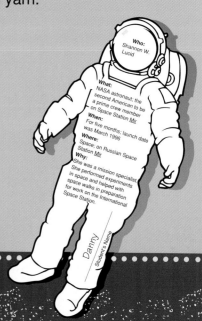

Who: Shannon W. Lucid

What: NASA astronaut; the second American to be a prime crew member on Space Station Mir

When: For five months; launch date was March 1996

Where: Space; on Russian Space Station Mir

Why: She was a mission specialist. She performed experiments in space and helped with space walks in preparation for work on the International Space Station.

Danny
Student's Name

The Man In The Moon

While man's first steps on the moon stand out as one of the finest achievements of our century, they unmasked the true nature of this small satellite. Our moon is really just a ball of rock and dust pockmarked by millions of meteorites that have plummeted through its thin atmosphere.

Share the moon facts below as you demonstrate the process that created the man-on-the-moon's face. First make play dough by mixing together one cup all-purpose flour, 1/2 cup salt, and 1/2 cup water plus two table-spoons. Blend well. (If you make the dough ahead of time, keep it sealed in plastic or in a lidded container.) Spread the dough in the bottom of an aluminum pie plate. Sprinkle 1/4 cup flour over the surface to represent the fine layer of moondust on the moon's surface. Dem-onstrate how a meteoroid falls from the sky and hits the lunar surface causing craters by placing the pie plate on the floor. Drop one marble or small ball onto the plate from shoulder height. Gently remove the marble and al-low students to examine the crater. Give each child an opportunity to make a crater. Then place the model on the counter to dry and become hard. Finally remove the loose flour and observe the craters. Point out that foot-prints made by astronauts will remain unchanged for cen-turies because there is no wind or atmosphere on the moon to disturb them.

Moon Facts
- The moon, our closest space neighbor, is only about 238,857 miles away.
- Its diameter is 2,160 miles. That's about the same distance as from Memphis, Tennessee, to San Francisco, California.
- The moon's gravity has an effect on the large bodies of water on our planet, causing tides. However its gravity is not strong enough to retain an atmosphere.
- The moon always shows the same face to the Earth because the rate of its spin is the same as the rate of its orbit around the Earth.

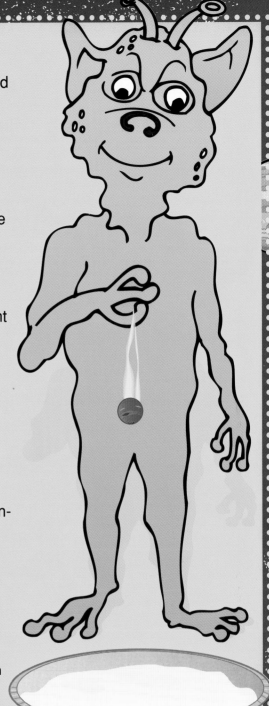

Sunseekers

Chase away January's chills by conducting a sun search. Give each pair of students a dictionary. Challenge each pair to find as many words as it can that contain *sun, sol-,* or *solar.* Each word must somehow relate to the sun (*solid* will not count). Designate a time limit and reward the winning pair with extra free time to brighten its day.

Fun With The Sun

Build this tasty model of the sun's layers to introduce your students to our closest star.

To Prepare: Before class bake a yellow cake in a large, round pan. Gather the following items: prepared yellow frosting, a small bag of little cinnamon candies, strips of red string licorice, red decorating sugar, a small bag of M&M's®, a small bag of coconut, and a spatula. Duplicate a class set of page 84. Write the following words on the board: *core, radiative zone, convection zone, photosphere, sunspots, chromosphere, spicules,* and *corona.* Make sure each student has a pencil, page 84, a box of crayons, and a hard surface on which to write.

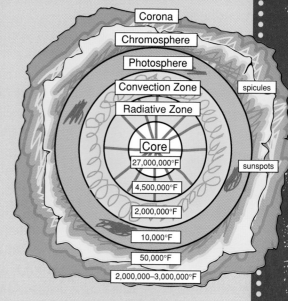

To Demonstrate: Place the cake and decorating materials on a table visible to students. As you spread the yellow frosting over the top of the cake, ask a student to share facts about the sun from the introduction on page 84. Next add the following decorations one at a time to illustrate the six layers of the sun (see the illustration):

1. **Core:** Sprinkle the cinnamon candies in a solid circle in the center of the cake.
2. **Radiative Zone:** Arrange red licorice strips so that they radiate out from the core.
3. **Convection Zone:** Sprinkle red sugar in a looping pattern to represent churning gases.
4. **Photosphere:** Place M&M's® (to represent sunspots) throughout this layer.
5. **Chromosphere:** Sprinkle coconut (to represent spicules) around this layer.
6. **Corona:** Leave this layer alone. Explain that the sun's corona does not actually end in a perfectly round sphere shape.

Each time you decorate one of the layers, share information about it from the chart on this page. Instruct each student to record these facts on his copy of page 84, then color each layer on his diagram according to your directions (also listed on the chart).

To Enjoy: After students have completed their diagrams, dig into this "sun-sational" treat, along with cups of orange juice.

No.	Name	Temperature	Interesting Feature	Coloring Directions
1	Core	27,000,000°F	The *thermonuclear* reactions taking place in this layer produce the sun's light and heat.	Use red to make lightning flashes.
2	Radiative Zone	4,500,000°F	The gases in this second layer are as dense as water.	Color this zone yellow with red lines passing through it from the core.
3	Convection Zone	2,000,000°F	Here gases churn violently, carrying energy toward the surface.	Color this zone yellow with orange-red loops swirling through it.
4	Photosphere	10,000°F	The *sunspots,* or cooler areas that can be seen from the Earth, radiate from here. This layer gives off the heat and light energy of the sun.	Color this layer orange with occasional dark brown spots to represent sunspots.
5	Chromosphere	50,000°F	Streams of gases, called *spicules,* shoot up from this layer of the sun's atmosphere.	Color this layer with red near the inner edge, orange in the middle, and yellow near the outer edge.
6	Corona	2,000,000–3,000,000°F	In this upper layer of the sun's atmosphere, gases expand away from the sun creating *solar wind.*	Color this layer with yellow near the inner edge, orange in the middle, and red near the outer edge.

The Right Stuff

What does it mean to have the "right stuff" to be an astronaut? Write four headings on the board: *Knowledge, Skills, Character Traits,* and *Other.* Have students brainstorm traits that they believe all astronauts should have. Then read excerpts from one or more of the books listed at the right. As you read, have a student volunteer record any other traits that were not previously mentioned.

I think I have the "right stuff" to be an astronaut because I am healthy, good at math, and I'm not afraid of heights!

Next have each student cut out and color a copy of the helmet pattern on page 85, then trace it onto a sheet of lined paper and cut out the tracing. Invite each student to write his thoughts about one or more of the questions at the right on the lined cutout. Have the student staple the helmet pattern over the written response and write his name on the helmet. Display these on a bulletin board titled "Do We Have The 'Right Stuff'?"

Questions:
- Would I make a good astronaut? Why or why not?
- What qualities do I possess that show that I have the right stuff to become an astronaut?
- Is there a NASA career that appeals to me? Which one and why?
- What would I like to achieve if I became an astronaut?
- Is there another career for which I think I have the right stuff? What is it?

Books To Use:
To Space And Back by Sally K. Ride and Susan Okie (Lothrop, Lee & Shepard Books; 1989)
Space Challenger: The Story Of Guion Bluford by James Haskins and Kathleen Benson (Carolrhoda Books, Inc.; 1984)
I'd Like To Be An…Astronaut by Kim Mitzo Thompson and Karen Mitzo Hilderbrand (Twin Sisters Productions, 1996)
How To Fly The Space Shuttle by Russell Shorto (John Muir Publications, 1992)
Space Camp®: The Great Adventure For NASA Hopefuls by Anne Baird (Morrow Junior Books, 1992)

Asteroid Obstacle Course

Combine a lesson about asteroids with some exercise and fun. Arrange Hula-Hoop® rings and/or cones in a wide, uneven circle. Point out that this circle represents the asteroid belt that revolves around the sun between Mars and Jupiter. Astronomers have counted thousands of asteroids within the belt.

Divide your class in half. Tell one half to become asteroids by spreading themselves among the hoops and cones in the circle. Have these students slowly weave their way in one direction within the belt. Instruct the other students to stand in the center of the circle and pretend to be spacecrafts trying to safely maneuver their way from Mars, through the asteroid belt, to Jupiter on the other side. Tell students that if a spacecraft touches or is touched by an asteroid (cone, hoop, or person) it becomes part of the belt. Once all of the spacecrafts have either crossed the belt or become asteroids, have the two groups switch roles and play again.

Astronaut Training

Astronauts must be physically fit to live and work in space. Conduct this fun and fast-moving physical workout to see if your students have the right stuff. Adjust the rate of exercise and allow for rest periods depending on the fitness of your students.

1. Stretches—Warm Up
   a. Plant your feet facing forward and about shoulder width apart. Reach up as high as you can, stretching onto your tiptoes. Slowly bring your arms down, bending your waist and knees till you can stretch your arms through your legs. Repeat five times.
   b. Plant your feet again. Make fists. Rotate your arms forward in big circles five times, then backward five times.
   c. Plant your feet. Reach your right arm over your head and stretch it to the left side. Switch arms and sides. Repeat each side five times.
   d. Plant your feet. Pull your knee up to your chest and hug it tightly. Count to five. Put your leg down. Do each leg five times.

2. The Frog (Squat Thrusts)
   Squat down with both hands on the floor on the sides of your knees. Shoot both legs backward together while keeping hands flat on the floor. Shoot legs back into the squat position. Repeat five times.

3. Jumping Jacks
   Do ten, rest for 15 seconds, then do ten more.

4. Knee Tag
   Plant your feet. Lift your right knee and tap it with your left elbow. Put your foot down. Lift your left knee and tap it with your right elbow. Put your foot down. Repeat ten times.

5. Running
   Run in place for three minutes without stopping and without leaving your spot.

6. Cool Down
   Repeat the stretching exercises above, doing each exercise three times each.

Net News

The United States, Russia, the European Space Agency, Japan, and Canada are working together to build the International Space Station. It's hoped that such a massive cooperative effort will help make the world a safer, more peaceful place. This station will conduct science research to benefit all humanity as well as make new discoveries about our Earth. Learn about this historic effort and other space-related news by linking your class to the NASA web site on the Internet. Use one of these two addresses: http://issa-www.jsc.nasa.gov/ **or** http://spacelink.msfc.nasa.gov/.

Student Name

ASTRONAUT

Act.:

Date:

Act.:

Date:

Act.:

Date:

Act.:

Date:

Act.:

Date:

Act.:

Date:

Act.:

Date:

Act.:

Date:

Act.:

Date:

Act.:

Date:

Act.:

Date:

Act.:

Date:

Wish You Were Here!

Vocabulary Strips

Use with "Extraterrestrial Terminology" on page 68.

air pressure	Force of the atmosphere pushing on the Earth
asteroids	Rocky bodies that orbit the sun mainly between Mars and Jupiter
astronaut	Person from the United States who travels outside the Earth's atmosphere
atmosphere	Layer of gases around a planet, star, or moon
axis	Imaginary line through the middle of a planet
chromosphere	Middle layer of the sun's atmosphere
colonization	Establishing a new community of inhabitants where they had not lived before
convection zone	Layer of sun just below the surface that carries energy to the surface
corona	Outermost layer of the sun's atmosphere
cosmonaut	Person from the former Soviet Union who travels outside the Earth's atmosphere
craters	Holes on a planet's or moon's surface, made by meteorites or volcanoes
force	A cause that changes an object's shape or motion
gravity	Force that pulls objects toward the Earth
habitat	Place where one lives; environment
lift	The force created by high and low air pressures, which get a plane off the ground
light speed	The speed at which light travels (186,000 miles per second)
lunar	Having to do with the moon
meteor	Tiny meteoroid or asteroid that has entered the Earth's atmosphere
meteorite	Meteoroid that has hit a planet's surface
meteoroid	Metallic or rocky matter drifting in space
Milky Way galaxy	The spiral group of stars, dust, and gas that contains our sun and planets of the solar system
NASA	National Aeronautics & Space Administration
nova & supernova	Exploding stars that become dim again
orbit	In space, the path one body takes around another
photosphere	The surface of the sun
pioneer	Person who explores the new/unknown
planetarium	A model of the solar system
radiative zone	Middle layer of the sun; draws heat from the center out to the convection zone
revolution	One full trip on an orbit
rotation	One full turn on an axis
satellite	A smaller body that orbits a larger body
science fiction	Imaginative stories about science
simulator	Device that creates conditions almost exactly like those one expects in an actual situation; usually used for testing and training
solar system	The sun and all of the planets and other bodies that orbit it
space shuttle	A reusable spacecraft controlled or piloted by astronauts
spicules	Streams of gas that shoot up from the chromosphere
sunspots	Dark patches on the sun's surface
telescope	Tool used to see the stars in our galaxy and beyond
terraforming	Altering a planet's atmosphere so that it can be inhabited by people from Earth
thrust	Forward-directed force
universe	Everything that we know exists and believe may exist
weight	Force of gravity placed on an object

The Weigh Of The Worlds

Part 1: Have you ever wanted to leap tall buildings in a single bound? If you lived on Mercury or Mars, you'd be able to jump almost three times higher than you can now. Complete column 3 in the chart below as you compare the weight of a 10-pound bag of apples to its weight on another planet or the moon.

Part 2: Measure your weight on the bathroom scale and record it in the fourth column in the Earth row. Use the formula below to figure out your weight on the other planets and our moon. For example, if you weigh 97 pounds on Earth and you want to learn your weight on Mercury, multiply 97 times 0.38. You'd weigh 36.86 pounds on Mercury.

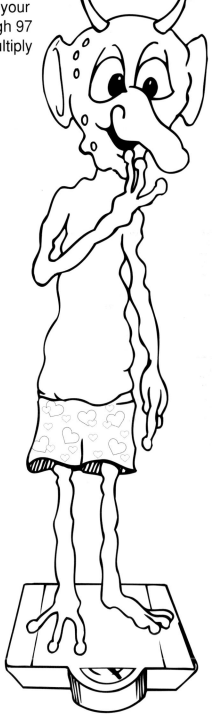

**your weight x the number in column 2 =
your weight on that planet or moon**

1 Planet/ Moon	2 Weight of one Earth- pound	3 Weight of one 10-lb. bag of apples	4 Your weight
Mercury	0.38 lb.	3.8 lb.	
Venus	0.9 lb.	9.0 lb.	
The Moon	0.16 lb.	1.6 lb.	
Earth	1.0 lb.	10.0 lb.	
Mars	0.38 lb.		
Jupiter	2.87 lb.		
Saturn	1.32 lb.		
Uranus	0.93 lb.		
Neptune	1.23 lb.		
Pluto	0.03 lb.		

Bonus Box: On the back of this paper, list the advantages and disadvantages of living in a place where you'd weigh only a third of your present weight.

Note To The Teacher: Use this page with "Gravity—A Weighty Matter" on page 69. You will need a bathroom scale for this activity.

My Very Educated Mother Just Served Us Nine Pizzas

Does the title above make any sense? It does if you're trying to memorize the order of the nine planets from the sun. The first letter of each word stands for a different planet. These planets travel in the same direction around the sun. Their *orbits,* or paths, lie in a flat plane except for Pluto's orbit, which is tilted. Each orbit is shaped like an elongated circle, or *ellipse.*

The chart below will help you make a model of the planets' orbits. Follow these steps to complete the chart (Saturn has been done as an example):

1. First divide Saturn's distance from the sun by 10 million. (Dividing by 10 million is the same as moving the decimal seven places to the left.) This will convert the distance to a more manageable scale *(88.82000000).*
2. Round this number to the nearest whole; then write this number in column 3 *(88.82000000 = 89).*
3. Pretend that each number represents inches. For instance, the distance from Saturn to the sun is now 89 inches.
4. Convert Saturn's inches in column 3 to feet and inches. Write these new numbers in column 4 *(89 ÷ 12 = 7 feet 5 inches).* If the number in column 3 is less than 12, just write it as inches in column 4.
5. Repeat steps 1 through 4 for the other eight planets.

1 Planet	2 Distance From The Sun (In Miles)	3 New Scale	4 Scale Converted To Feet/Inches	
			ft.	in.
Mercury	35,980,000.0			
Venus	67,230,000.0			
Earth	92,960,000.0			
Mars	141,000,000.0			
Jupiter	483,600,000.0			
Saturn	888,200,000.0	*89*	*7*	*5*
Uranus	1,786,400,000.0			
Neptune	2,798,800,000.0			
Pluto	3,666,200,000.0			

Bonus Box: The title above is called a *mnemonic phrase.* Think of another mnemonic phrase that will help you memorize the order of the nine planets. Write it on the back of this page.

Note To The Teacher: Use this page with "Seeing Is Believing" on page 70. Be sure that students understand that because a planet's orbit is elliptical—not circular—the numbers in the "Distance From The Sun" column vary. The numbers given are the mean distances from the sun.

You Look Young For Your Age!

If you like getting lots of birthday presents, you should consider living on Mercury! On Earth you celebrate a birthday every 365 days—the same length of time it takes our planet to make one revolution around the sun. But if you lived on Mercury you'd celebrate a birthday every 88 days. Why? Because it only takes Mercury 88 days to revolve once around the sun.

Complete the information on the cake below. First figure out your age in Earth-days. To do this, multiply your age by 365; then write that number on the top of the cake in the blank. Next figure out your age on the other planets. To do this, use a calculator to divide your age in Earth-days by the number of days in one revolution for each planet (see the chart). Round each number to the nearest whole number, tenth, or hundredth.

EXAMPLE: If you are 6 years old, you have lived 6 x 365 days, or 2,190 days. Divide 2,190 days by 88 days (length of one year on Mercury). The rounded answer is 25 years.

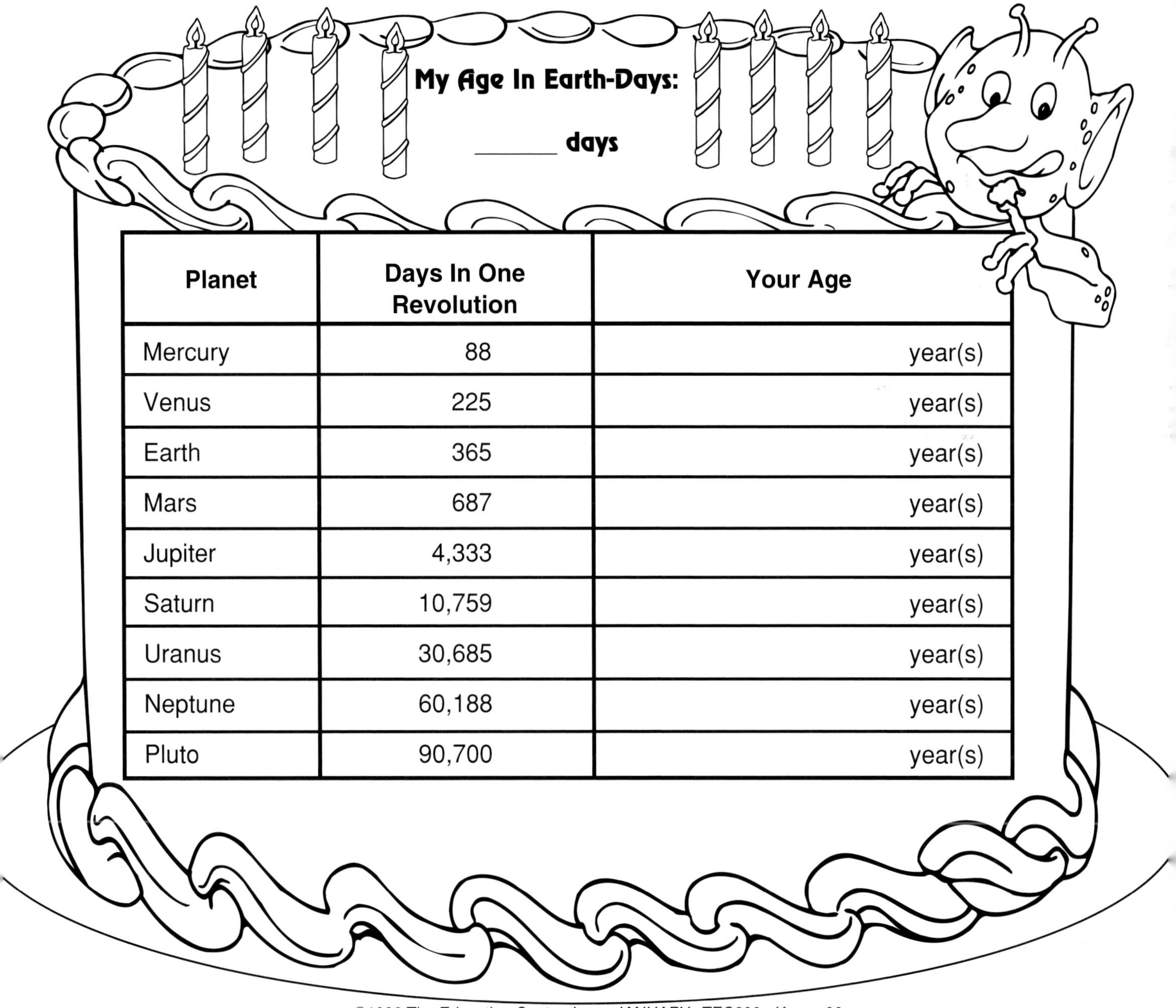

My Age In Earth-Days:

_____ days

Planet	Days In One Revolution	Your Age	
Mercury	88		year(s)
Venus	225		year(s)
Earth	365		year(s)
Mars	687		year(s)
Jupiter	4,333		year(s)
Saturn	10,759		year(s)
Uranus	30,685		year(s)
Neptune	60,188		year(s)
Pluto	90,700		year(s)

Note To The Teacher: Use this page with "All In One Year" on page 70. Provide students with calculators.

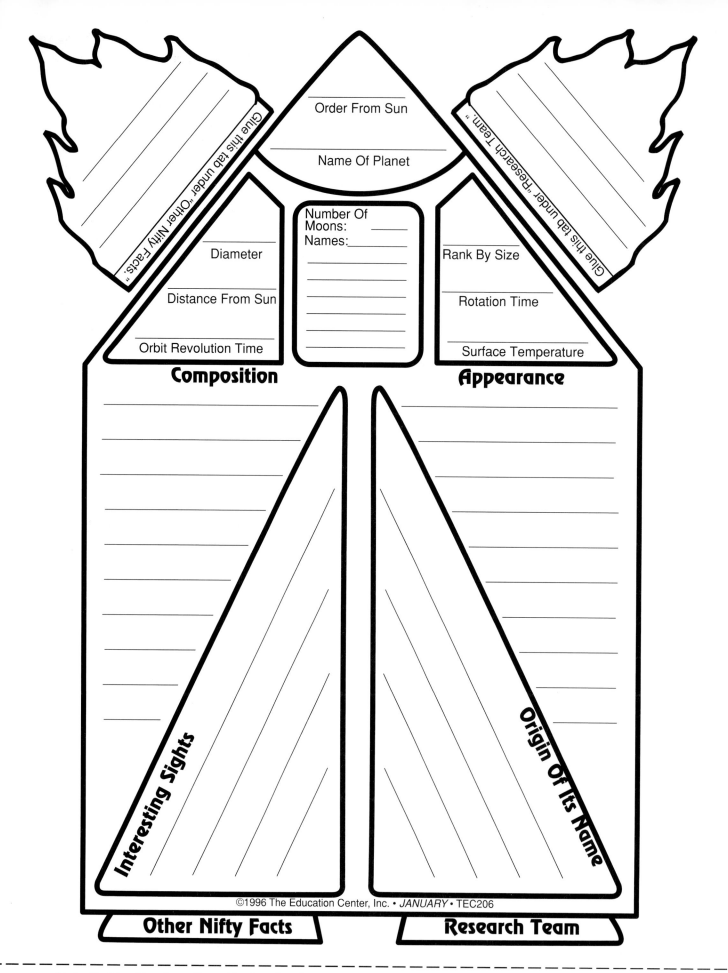

Order From Sun

Name Of Planet

Glue this tab under "Other Nifty Facts."

Glue this tab under "Research Team."

Number Of Moons: _____
Names: _____

Diameter

Distance From Sun

Orbit Revolution Time

Rank By Size

Rotation Time

Surface Temperature

Composition

Appearance

Interesting Sights

Origin Of Its Name

©1996 The Education Center, Inc. • JANUARY • TEC206

Other Nifty Facts

Research Team

Note To The Teacher: Use with "Satellite Savvy" on page 71. Students will need access to reference materials. They will also need scissors and glue.

82

Who:

What:

When:

Where:

Why:

Student's Name

©1996 The Education Center, Inc.

Name Of Moon:

Parent Planet:

Moon Facts:

©1996 The Education Center, Inc.

Use with "Moonstruck" on page 71.

Our Great Ball Of Fire!

At a distance of about 93 million miles from Earth, the sun is the closest star to our planet. It is in the center of our solar system. It pulls all the planets into orbit with its powerful gravity. On the lines, write facts about the sun as your teacher creates a model of its layers. Include the name of each layer, its temperature, and any interesting facts.

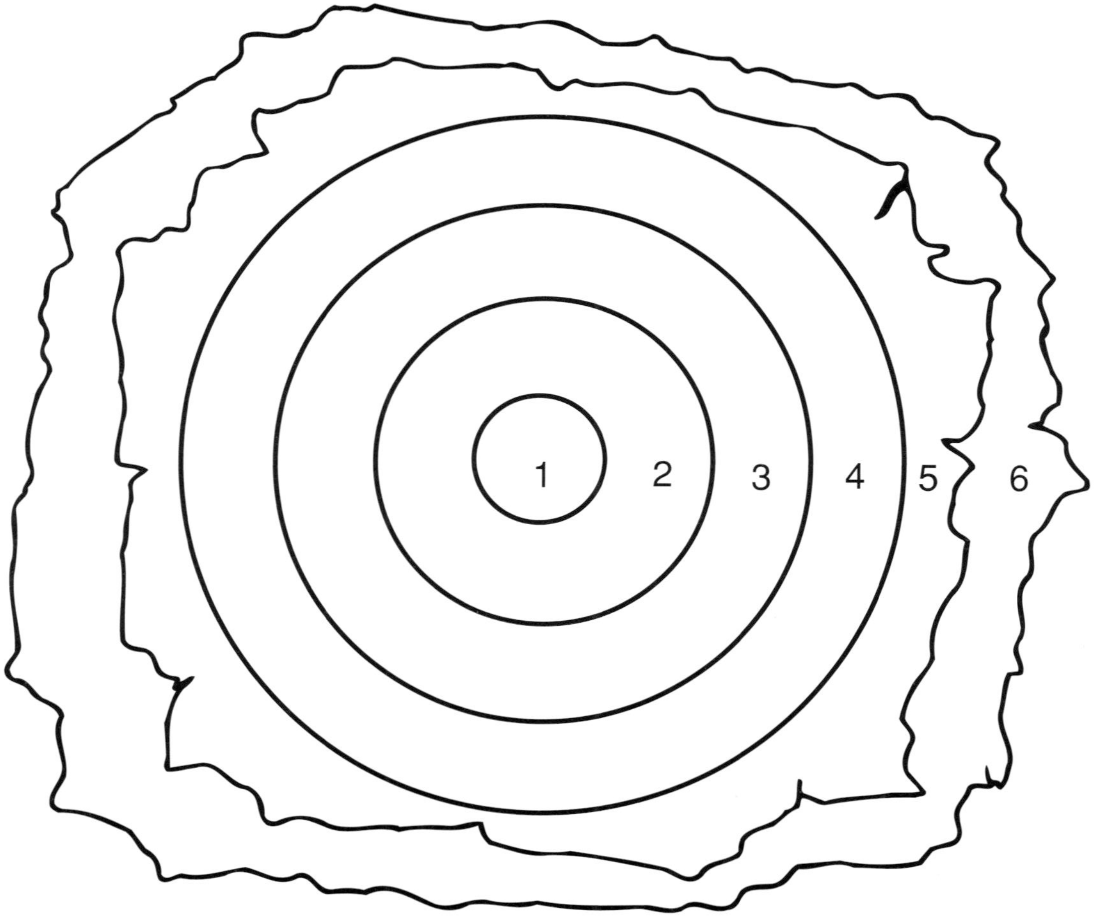

1. Name: _____
   Temperature: _____
   Other Facts: _____

2. Name: _____
   Temperature: _____
   Other Facts: _____

3. Name: _____
   Temperature: _____
   Other Facts: _____

4. Name: _____
   Temperature: _____
   Other Facts: _____

5. Name: _____
   Temperature: _____
   Other Facts: _____

6. Name: _____
   Temperature: _____
   Other Facts: _____

©1996 The Education Center, Inc. • JANUARY • TEC206 • Key p. 96

Note To The Teacher: Use this page with "Fun With The Sun" on page 74. Students will need crayons to color the diagram according to your directions.

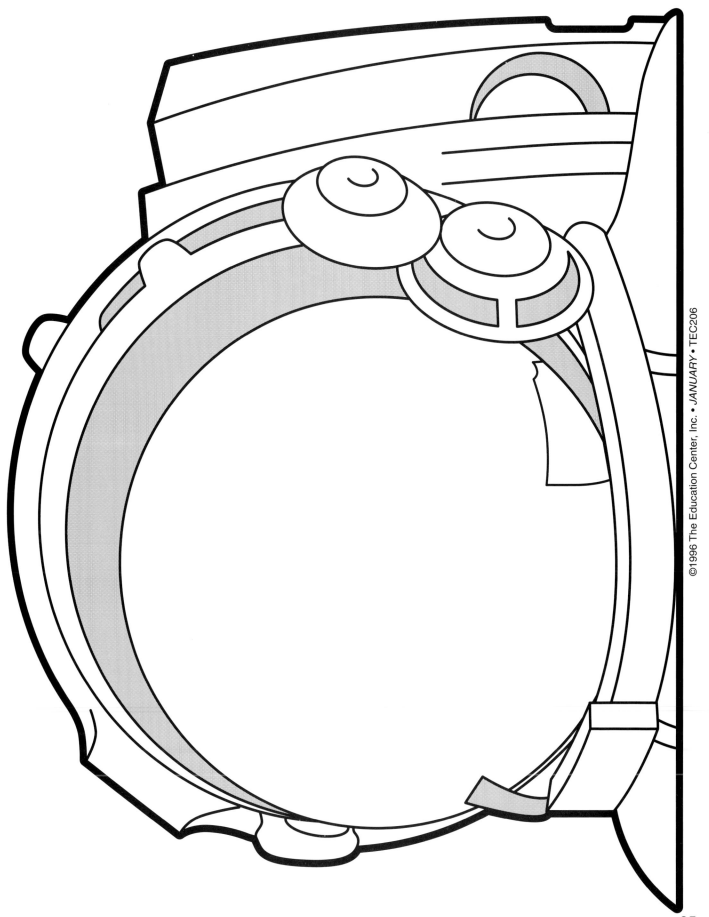

On Your Mark, Get Set, THINK!

Puzzles And Brainteasers To **Stretch** The Mind

Celebrate National Puzzle Day (January 29) with this collection of fun puzzles, brainteasers, and mental exercises.

by Irving Crump and Ann Fisher

Building The Mind Muscle

Solving puzzles, riddles, and brainteasers is an excellent way for students to develop divergent thinking and problem-solving skills. The success in solving a puzzle is often based on *how* the solver thinks about the puzzle, rather than natural ability or intelligence. So students who may not be as academically gifted as their classmates can often experience success when solving puzzles.

Set up a puzzle corner or minicenter in your classroom. Feature a different puzzle in the center every two to three days, and challenge each student to work either independently or with a partner to solve it. Invite students and their parents to contribute their own favorite puzzles for the class to solve. Begin a file of your favorites to use from year to year.

Four By Fours

Materials needed: a deck of playing cards for every six students

Provide each pair of students with 16 playing cards: the four suits of any four ranks. For example, provide one pair with all of the jacks, queens, kings, and aces; another pair with all of the twos, threes, fours, and fives; and a third pair with all of the sixes, sevens, eights, and nines. Instruct each pair of students to arrange its 16 cards in a 4 x 4 array so that each row and each column has exactly one card of each rank. A solution is shown above, but there are many more.

- After students have met the first challenge, have them make an array in which the diagonals, as well as the rows and columns, all contain only one card of each rank.
- Last have each pair of students find a solution in which there is only one card of each suit as well as only one card of each rank in every row, column, and diagonal. (Share with students that there are dozens of solutions!)

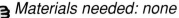

100 Adds Up!

Materials needed: none

Review basic addition facts with this fun game of strategy. Divide students into pairs. If you have an odd number of students, ask a volunteer to be your partner. Begin with the first player calling out a number from 1 to 10. The second player then adds any number from 1 to 10 to the number that Player 1 chose. Play continues alternately by increasing the last sum by any amount from 1 to 10. The object of the game is to be the first person to reach exactly 100.

Play several rounds, mixing players with new partners. After playing three or four games, challenge students to define the strategy to use to win every game. (See the key on page 96 for the winning strategy.)

Tumbler Stumpers

Materials needed: six similar plastic tumblers, water

- Line up six tumblers as shown—the first three tumblers filled halfway with water and the last three empty. The challenge for students? Rearrange the glasses so that the first one has water, the second one is empty, the third has water, the fourth is empty, the fifth has water, and the sixth one is empty. However, only *one* glass can be moved. (Although this seems impossible, the solution is quite simple. See the key on page 96.)

- Arrange three tumblers as shown—the first one upside down, the second one right-side up, and the third upside down. The challenge for students: In three moves—not one—turn the glasses so that all three are right-side up. In addition, two glasses must be moved during each move, one per hand. (For the solution, see the key on page 96.)

What's Your Birth-*day*?

Materials needed: pencil and paper for each student

Few students could probably tell you the day of the week on which they were born. By following the steps below, each student can determine the day on which he or she entered the world. A sample birthdate—May 12, 1986—is computed below.

1. Let A be the *year* in which you were born.
   A = 1986
2. Let B be the *day of the year* you were born.
   January: 31 days
   February: 28 days (1986 was not a leap year.)
   March: 31 days
   April: 30 days
   May: 12 days
   B = 132nd day of the year (31 + 28 + 31, etc.)
   B = 132
3. Find C: C = (A − 1) ÷ 4 and ignore the remainder.
   C = 496
4. Find D: D = A + B + C
   D = 2,614
5. Divide D by 7 and note the remainder: 373 r. 3

Use the table below to see which day of the week corresponds to the remainder of the division problem in step 5. (A student born on May 12, 1986, was born on a Monday.)

Remainder:	Birthday:
0	Fri.
1	Sat.
2	Sun.
3	Mon.
4	Tue.
5	Wed.
6	Thur.

The Tower Of Brahma

Materials needed: one dime, penny, nickel, and quarter for each student

The Tower of Brahma is an age-old game with roots in an ancient Hindu legend. The legend says that in a certain temple there is a brass plate into which are fixed three pins. On one pin, at the beginning of time, there were 64 disks. The largest disk rested on the brass plate. The remainder were stacked on top of it in gradual descending size up to the smallest one, the 64th, on top. Every day and night, a priest transfers the disks from the first pin to the third pin—at the rate of one per second—never allowing a disk to be placed on top of a smaller one. He uses the middle pin as a temporary storage site. One day, the original tower will be rebuilt with all 64 disks in correct order on the third pin. And that day will be the end of the earth.

Have students simulate this game by first using three disks: a dime, penny, and nickel. On a piece of paper, have each student draw three circles and label them 1, 2, and 3. Next have each student stack the three coins on the first circle: the nickel on the bottom, then the penny, and then the dime on top. Tell students that the object of the game is to move the stack of coins from the first circle to the third circle, one at a time. The second circle can serve as a temporary storage site, and a coin can never be placed on one that is smaller in size. What is the fewest number of moves in which this can be accomplished? *(7 moves: D-3, P-2, D-2, N-3, D-1, P-3, D-3)* Have students record their moves on paper.

Next have students play the game as described but with four coins: a dime, penny, nickel, and quarter. The object is to move the stack of four coins from the first circle to the third circle, one at a time, without ever placing a large coin on a smaller one. What is the fewest number of moves in which this can be accomplished? *(15: D-2, P-3, D-3, N-2, D-1, P-2, D-2, Q-3, D-3, P-1, D-1, N-3, D-2, P-3, D-3)*

Now back to the Hindu legend. Just how long will it take to move 64 disks from one pin to another, at the rate of one per second? There's no need to worry about the earth coming to an end anytime soon, because it will take 585,000 million years!

Tied Up

Materials: two 3-foot pieces of string or yarn for each pair of students

Students don't have to be gymnasts to unravel this puzzle. Provide each student with a 3-foot piece of string or yarn; then divide students into pairs. If you have an odd number of students, ask a volunteer to be your partner. First have students tie their strings to their wrists as shown in the diagram: Student B first ties the ends of a string to Student A's wrists. Student A then ties one end of the piece of string to Student B's left wrist, loops the string under and over his own string, then ties the other end to Student B's right wrist.

Now the challenge: Each pair of students must separate themselves from each other without untying or cutting the string. Each student's wrists will still be connected, but the pair will not be intertwined. See the key on page 96 for a solution.

Magic Numbers

Materials: copies of the diagrams below drawn on a transparency or chalkboard

The magic square is probably the oldest math puzzle in existence. Some examples have been found that date back to before 2,000 B.C.! But other shapes can also be used. Challenge students with the following puzzles based on "magic numbers." Solutions are listed on page 96.

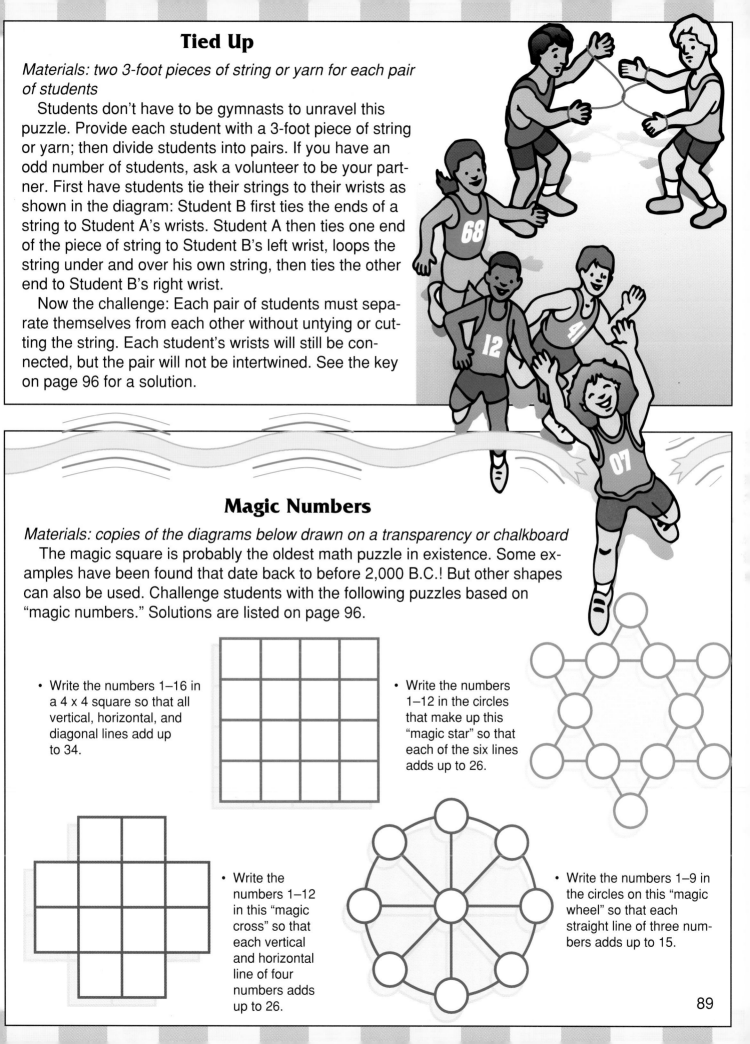

- Write the numbers 1–16 in a 4 x 4 square so that all vertical, horizontal, and diagonal lines add up to 34.

- Write the numbers 1–12 in the circles that make up this "magic star" so that each of the six lines adds up to 26.

- Write the numbers 1–12 in this "magic cross" so that each vertical and horizontal line of four numbers adds up to 26.

- Write the numbers 1–9 in the circles on this "magic wheel" so that each straight line of three numbers adds up to 15.

89

Square Sums

Everybody loves a good number puzzle! Here's a pair that may keep you busy for awhile. Dive in!

1. Cut out the 15 markers at the bottom of this page. Place markers **1–10** in the circles so that the four corners of each square add up to **22.** To help get you started, place the 7 marker in the circle labeled 7. Draw your solution on an other sheet of paper.

2. Now use the markers numbered **6–15.** Place the markers in the circles so that the four corners of each square add up to **42.** To help get you started, place the 12 marker on top of the circled 7. Draw your solution on another sheet of paper.

Bonus Box: Can you make five 5's equal 100? Use any operations or groupings of the fives.

Alphabet Antics

There are lots of great word puzzles that use all 26 letters in our alphabet. But here's one that uses the shortest alphabet in the world! The language *Rotokas* of central Bougainville Island, Papua New Guinea, has only 11 letters:

a b e g i k o p r t u

On another sheet of paper, list words of four letters or more that can be made using only the 11 letters above. You may repeat letters within a word. For example, *treat* would be okay.

Next look for and circle your words and others in the word search below. Words may appear horizontally, vertically, or diagonally, in any direction. To make your job a little easier, find words that have only 4–6 letters each. (Hint: There are more than 80 words.)

r	e	t	t	u	g	e	t	e	p	o	r	g	k
a	e	g	i	e	b	k	t	r	t	u	o	r	t
e	t	g	e	u	u	o	t	a	e	i	a	e	p
b	a	k	r	r	t	p	a	g	e	e	r	e	e
r	e	g	a	e	u	e	p	g	p	o	u	t	e
e	b	i	r	t	t	o	e	e	i	r	a	k	k
p	o	r	t	i	k	r	p	b	r	o	k	e	a
r	k	e	k	a	r	b	o	p	g	r	e	k	r
e	r	r	t	e	p	i	k	o	k	r	p	e	g
k	e	i	t	i	i	g	o	t	p	e	o	t	r
a	t	t	o	i	r	g	o	t	e	t	k	u	a
e	u	k	o	t	t	e	r	e	e	i	e	o	t
b	o	o	k	a	e	r	b	r	b	b	r	r	e

Bonus Box: Can you list 20 words of just three letters each using the alphabet described above? Do not repeat letters within a word. List the words on the back of this page.

Does This Compute?

Many puzzles are created by computer, but here's a puzzle *about* computers! Each letter of the alphabet has been given a value from 1 to 26 as shown on the keys. At the bottom of this page are 12 computer terms, each with two missing letters. To figure out which letters are missing, you need to add the value of the letters that are given, subtract that sum from the word's total value, and then find letters that match the difference to complete the word. Study the example below the keyboard.

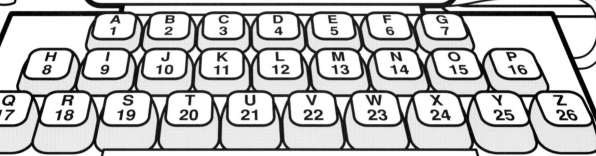

A 1	B 2	C 3	D 4	E 5	F 6	G 7
H 8	I 9	J 10	K 11	L 12	M 13	N 14	O 15	P 16
Q 17	R 18	S 19	T 20	U 21	V 22	W 23	X 24	Y 25	Z 26

D + A + ___ + ___ = 26

1. The value of *D* (4) plus *A* (1) is 5.
2. Subtract 5 from the word total: 26 − 5 = 21.
3. The two missing letters must add up to 21.
4. Think of a term that might work.
5. *DATE* might work, but its total (30) is too high.
6. How about *DATA,* which has a total value of 26?
7. So the solutions are *T* and *A,* which make the computer-related word *DATA.*

---

1. I + ___ + ___ + U + T = 80

2. D + ___ + S + ___ = 43

3. M + O + ___ + ___ + E = 73

4. P + ___ + I + N + ___ = 77

5. ___ + O + D + ___ + M = 50

6. C + ___ + I + ___ + S = 55

7. B + Y + ___ + ___ = 52

8. V + I + ___ + ___ + S = 89

9. ___ + C + O + ___ = 41

10. S + ___ + R + ___ + E + N = 64

11. M + E + ___ + O + ___ + Y = 89

12. S + ___ + S + ___ + E + M = 101

Bonus Box: Find the total value of the word *programming:* _____. Can you think of a computer term that has a higher value? Write it on the back of this page.

Two-Letter Clues

Crossword fans quickly learn many unusual words to help them solve their favorite puzzles, including some very strange, very short words. In each section of the puzzle below is a pair of letters. If the letter pair forms a real word, color that space with a crayon or colored pencil. If the pair is not a real word, leave its section blank.

Keep a dictionary handy; the answers may surprise you! If you color in all the right sections, a familiar word will appear.

As you look up words, find one that will fit each definition below. Write the word in the blank.

1. Greek letters _____
2. an urban railway _____
3. sweetheart _____
4. bone _____
5. thanks _____
6. a form of "mother" _____
7. a form of "father" _____
8. a tool _____
9. an animal _____
10. a greeting _____

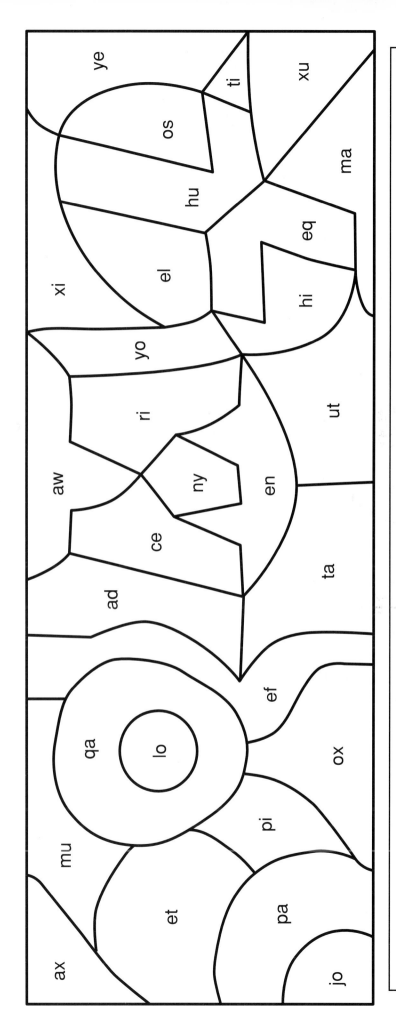

Bonus Box: Find the words in the colored sections of the puzzle that would come first and last in alphabetical order. Circle the first word. Draw a box around the last word.

Three Thought-Provoking Thrillers

Cut out the pieces of each puzzle below. Then follow the directions to complete each one.

Puzzle 1
A Trying Triangle

Arrange the three trapezoids to make an equilateral triangle. (All three sides are equal.)

Puzzle 2
Four = Five? No Way!

Arrange the four trees to make five.

Puzzle 3
A "Te-rrific" Challenge

Arrange the four puzzle pieces to make a perfect capital *T*.

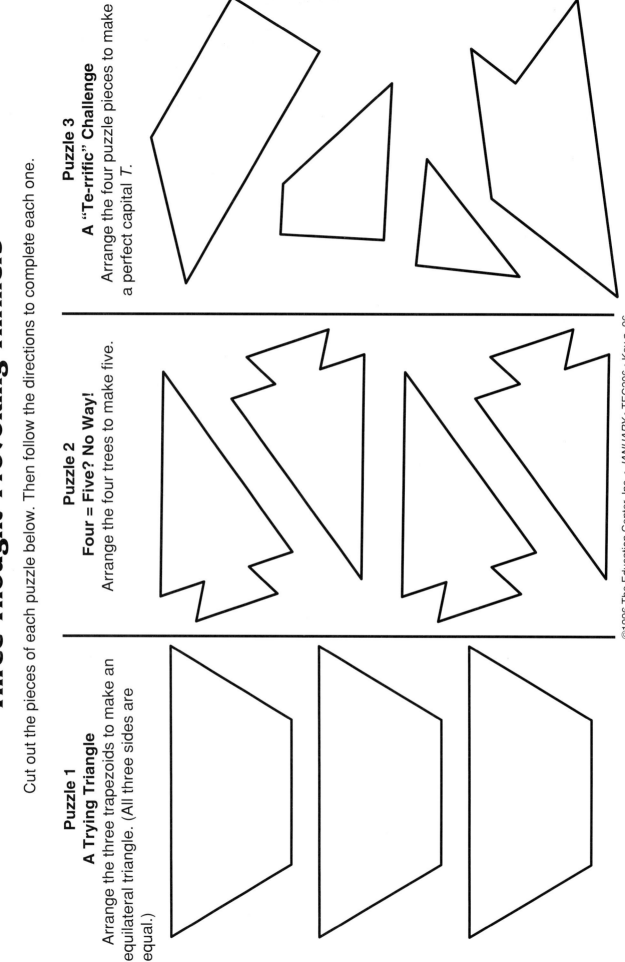

Answer Keys

Page 44
Exact wording may vary.

7:00 A.M.—Eat breakfast with family
7:30 A.M.—Work on church business
8:00 A.M.—Agree to speak to school group
8:30 A.M.—Meet with leaders to plan boycott
10:00 A.M.—Be interviewed on phone
10:30 A.M.—Meet with lawyers about boycott
12:00 P.M.—Have lunch with boycott leaders
1:00 P.M.—Help arrange cars for car pool
2:00 P.M.—Speak to school group about boycott
3:00 P.M.—Have second meeting with lawyers
4:30 P.M.—Return phone calls about boycott
5:00 P.M.—Read notes for speech
6:00 P.M.—Eat dinner with family
7:00 P.M.—Deliver speech about boycott
8:00 P.M.—Visit hospitalized church members

Page 56
Here are possible ways to paraphrase the four sections of the Declaration Of Independence:

Part I: Introduction—Sometimes people in a group find that they have to break away from the country they once belonged to. They find that they have no choice but to become a separate nation with the same powers and rights as other countries. When a group chooses to do this, it shows respect to others by explaining its reasons.

Part II: Beliefs—We believe that God has given everyone basic rights that no one can take away. These rights make all people equal. They include the right to live, the right to be free, and the right to be happy.

Part III: Wrongs—(In this section Jefferson cited more than 25 ways the king of England had wronged the Americans. Students should be able to write two or three in their own words.)
- The king has not let colonies pass their own laws.
- The king has not given the colonies representation in Parliament.
- The king has forced colonists to house (quarter) soldiers in their homes.

Part IV: Conclusion—We, the United States of America, are now a free and independent nation. We are no longer ruled by England. As a free country, we can make peace or war and do business with other countries. We now have the same rights as other countries.

Page 58
The coded message is:

"Listen, my children, and you shall hear
Of the midnight ride of Paul Revere,
On the eighteenth of April, in Seventy-five;
Hardly a man is now alive
Who remembers that famous day and year."
—by Henry Wadsworth Longfellow

Page 66
	Estimate		Exact Total		
1.	$13.00	Exact Total:	$14.15	Change Due:	$.85
2.	$10.00	Exact Total:	$9.69	Change Due:	$.31
3.	$6.00	Exact Total:	$5.25	Money Needed:	$.25
4.	$15.00	Exact Total:	$7.50	Change Due:	$1.75
5.	$24.00	Exact Total:	$18.32	Change Due:	$1.68
6.	$18.00	Exact Total:	$14.50	Change Due:	$.50
7.	$12.00	Exact Total:	$11.34	Money Needed:	$1.34
8.	$6.00	Exact Total:	$5.15	Money Needed:	$.40
9.	$7.00	Exact Total:	$6.76	Change Due:	$1.24
10.	$5.00	Exact Total:	$4.23	Change Due:	$.52

Page 79
Students' weights will vary. Figures for column 3 are:
Mars—3.8 lb.
Jupiter—28.7 lb.
Saturn—13.2 lb.
Uranus—9.3 lb.
Neptune—12.3 lb.
Pluto—0.3 lb.

Page 80
Planet	New Scale	Feet	Inches
Mercury	4.0	0	4
Venus	7.0	0	7
Earth	9.0	0	9
Mars	14.0	1	2
Jupiter	48.0	4	0
Saturn	89.0	7	5
Uranus	179.0	14	11
Neptune	280.0	23	4
Pluto	367.0	30	7

Page 84
Answers may vary.
1. Core
   27,000,000°F
   The *thermonuclear* reactions that take place in this layer produce the sun's light and heat.

2. Radiative Zone
   4,500,000°F
   The gases in this second layer are as dense as water.

3. Convection Zone
   2,000,000°F
   Here gases churn violently, carrying energy toward the surface.

4. Photosphere
   10,000°F
   The *sunspots,* or cooler areas that can be seen from the Earth, radiate from here. This layer gives off the heat and light energy of the sun.

5. Chromosphere
   50,000°F
   Streams of gases, called *spicules,* shoot up from this layer.

6. Corona
   2,000,000–3,000,000°F
   In this upper layer of the sun's atmosphere, gases expand away from the sun creating *solar wind.*

Answer Keys

Page 87
100 Adds Up!

The key to reaching 100 first is to call 89 first. Then, no matter what your opponent adds to 89—1 through 10—you will win the game. In order to reach 89, you should try to call 78. Then regardless of what your opponent adds to 78, you will be able to reach 89. In order to reach 78, you must call 67. This pattern of backing up by 11 continues to 56, 45, 34, 23, and 12. So if a player is able to call out any of these numbers, he can be assured of reaching 100 first.

Tumbler Stumpers

- The second glass (the middle one with water) should be picked up and poured into the fifth (the middle empty one). Thus only one glass was moved, and now every other glass has water.

- First turn over glasses 1 and 2. Then turn over glasses 1 and 3. Last turn over glasses 1 and 2.

Page 89
Tied Up

Pass the loop of one string through the loop that encircles one of the second person's wrists, slide it over the hand, and pass it back again through the loop. The strings should now be separated.

Magic Numbers

16	3	2	13
5	10	11	8
9	6	7	12
4	15	14	1

	12	9	
2	7	6	11
5	3	10	8
	4	1	

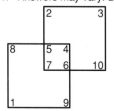

Page 90

1. Answers may vary. Below is one solution:

2. Answers may vary. Below is one solution:

Bonus Box answer:
One possible solution is (5 x 5 x 5) − (5 x 5) = 100.

Page 91
Words are listed by the appearance of their first letters, beginning in row 1.

row 1:	row 4:	row 6:	row 8:	row 10:	row 13:
regret	bear	beat	kite	took	book
tier	rube	rare	riot	poor	butte
gutter	retro	tribe	rake	error	butter
tree	tote	troop	brake	rate	beak
roar	page	tutu	bigger		beaker
rope	poke	aura	potter	row 11:	
grope	putt	keep	grip	tire	outer
greet	putter		gripe	rite	break
	rite	row 7:	goat	riot	brook
row 2:		port	grout	terror	beep
beige	row 5:	pour	rake		bite
burg	grub	beet		row 12:	rout
tote	eager	beggar	row 9:	utter	route
rout	utter	broke	riot	otter	
trout	pout	ripe	tire	trip	
	pear		otter	rook	
row 3:	trite		opter		
upper			rout		
tape			reek		
peek			poke		
			poker		
			grate		

Bonus Box answers: Answers may vary. Below are 30 suggestions:

age	pot	get	bag	tab	oak
ear	apt	rot	gut	big	toe
per	gap	art	rut	kit	bog
ape	put	got	beg	tap	out
gab	ark	rub	irk	bit	top

Page 92

1. input
2. disk
3. mouse
4. print
5. modem
6. chips
7. byte
8. virus
9. icon
10. screen
11. memory
12. system

Bonus Box answer: *programming* = 131. Two other words with higher values include *microcomputer* with 169 and *microprocessor* with 186. Students may also find others.

Page 93
All of the sections of the picture should be shaded except the ones containing *qa, ce, ny, ri, hu,* and *eq.* All of the others are real words. When the picture is turned upside down, the word *two* is visible.

1. mu, pi, or xi
2. el
3. jo
4. os
5. ta
6. ma
7. pa
8. ax
9. ox
10. hi

Bonus Box answers: *ad* (short for advertisement) and *yo* (used to call attention, to express affirmation)

Page 94

1.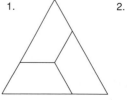

2.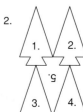

3.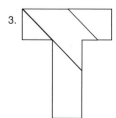

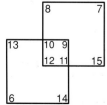